Dear Am.
So nice to see you again today.

*[signature]*
6.9.13

## Let Go

$6

# Let Go

Linda Xu

Copyright © 2013, Linda Xu

All rights reserved. No part of this book may be reproduced, stored, or transmitted by any means—whether auditory, graphic, mechanical, or electronic—without written permission of both publisher and author, except in the case of brief excerpts used in critical articles and reviews. Unauthorized reproduction of any part of this work is illegal and is punishable by law.

Paperback ISBN: 978-1-300-57558-0

Hardcover ISBN: 978-1-300-57559-7

# Contents

Prologue ................................................................... vii

Bliss in a Storm ............................................................ 1

Anything for Love ........................................................ 29

Betrayal ................................................................... 77

Let Go .................................................................... 157

# Prologue

The year was 1966, and the Cultural Revolution had just been officially launched. Throngs of young demonstrators holding giant portraits of Chairman Mao, beating drums and shouting slogans against his perceived enemies occupied the streets of Shanghai. This political movement was to quickly grow into a full-fledged violent factional struggle with millions of people to be persecuted and forced to endure a wide range of abuses including public humiliation, imprisonment, torture, harassment, and seizure of property. All that makes for human dignity was buried.

A petite and exhausted woman laid in one of the small beds in a crowded hospital ward, sweating profusely and groaning in pain, her bulging belly looked like it was going to pop. The unusually sultry and steamy July afternoon even by the Shanghai standard made everything hot to the touch. Between her contractions, she stared blankly outside the window, wondering how her husband, thousands of miles away in Yun Nan, was handling the hostility and mounting pressure that surrounded him.

Dusk didn't bring any relief from the heat wave. The air was unbearably stiff as the ground relinquished the heat it had soaked in all day long. The woman tossed and turned in anguish, her contractions peaked one after the other. Her baby was ready to make her entrance into a world that had been turned upside down.

"Another girl …" the woman moaned after one glance at her crying baby and then handed the baby over to her mother who was standing by her bed.

"What a gorgeous baby!" Grandma exclaimed admiringly. "Look at those long eye lashes … and her little high-bridged nose … she is going to be a beaut!"

"Well, poor little thing! Beaut or not, she is born at the wrong time." The woman sighed and looked away.

The baby continued to scream at the top of her lungs, waving her little fists frantically in the air. Grandma gently tickled her little palm with her index finger, and the baby girl held onto the finger as if her life were dependent on it and suddenly stopped crying.

The mother of the baby started to run a high fever after giving birth and remained sick for the next several weeks. Forty-two days later, her maternity leave was up, and she had to return to her job in Yun Nan. She handed her tiny baby girl to her mother again, and with a trembling voice said, "Mom, please take care of her for me."

"I will. Don't you worry about a thing, okay?" Grandma received the baby with a frowned smile. She had no idea where she and the baby were going to live.

# Bliss in a Storm

I woke up to the sound of a few little knocks on the door. "Mommy, can we watch TV?"

"Sure, baby. I'll be up soon to make us breakfast."

I looked at the clock: 7 a.m. I'd hosted a Thanksgiving dinner at our house last night. Since our families live in China, Thanksgiving dinner is usually a gathering of friends mostly from church. It was after midnight after I cleaned up and finally went to bed. I was tired still, my feet heavy from standing all day cooking and cleaning. I rolled over to face Joe. "Morning, baby!" I got my usual morning greeting.

"Morning! Tell me something. Why do kids always wake up at the same time no matter how late they go to sleep?" I moved closer to cuddle up in his arms.

"It is the work of their biological clock, the law of nature." He cleared his throat loudly. Joe is a noisy guy with all sorts of allergies and respiratory problems.

"When do we get to sleep in late and go out for brunch at let's say noon?"

He kissed me and whispered, "That may happen someday, baby, someday."

"Time for mommy to get up," I announced.

Once up, it would be non-stop for the rest of the day

I went to the bathroom, pulled my favorite no-longer-so-white Lands' End bathrobe off the hook at the back of the door and put it over my silky grey pajamas then went downstairs to the kitchen. Jane and Michelle were comfortably lying on the light-brown sectional sofa in the family room in front of the TV, eyes glued to the screen.

I pulled up the leaf gold cordless cellular shade in the kitchen. The morning sun made everything glow. The smell of the food from last night lingered. My kitchen was between the family and living rooms. It had plenty of counter space plus a central island. The cabinets were made of cheap dark wood. The house was twenty-five years old, and the kitchen could definitely use a facelift.

I made scrambled eggs for the girls. Joe's breakfast was easier to fix. He always had an apple, a bagel, and a cup of tea. As I was peeling an apple for Joe, something struck me like a lightening bolt. *I haven't had my period yet. I am never late! Oh, my God, I hope I'm not pregnant.* My heart started racing. The blood rushed to my head. *There's no reason to panic yet,* I assured myself. *I'll find out, then maybe I'll panic.*

After breakfast, I asked Joe to play a card game with girls so I could go to the supermarket. Then he did his usual dance in front of me, moving his body from side to side. Normally I'd laugh at his awkward movements, but I just smiled and headed to the garage.

I actually only needed one thing from the supermarket: the home pregnancy test. It took me a few minutes to get to the right aisle. I also picked up a few other things like milk and apples. On the way out, I slipped the test in my purse and put the rest of the stuff in the trunk.

When I got home, Jane and Michelle were drawing in the kitchen, and Joe was in his study room. I decided that this would be the perfect time to run the test. I was not good at waiting. I took the pregnancy test out of my purse, quietly sneaked into the bathroom of the master bedroom, and locked the door.

It had been a long while since I last ran a home pregnancy test. This thing looked different from what I remembered, and it claimed it could detect pregnancy three days before one missed her period. I followed each step in the instruction, flushed the toilet, laid the test next to the sink, and washed my hands. In two minutes I would know the result. I looked at my gold rectangular Seiko watch Joe gave for my birthday. It was 9:15 a.m. Time seemed to freeze. The smell of lavender was in the air. It must be from the shampoo Joe used for his morning shower. I looked up and saw my reflection in the large mirror: large brown eyes, a high-bridged nose, not a common Asian feature, thin-lipped mouth, my face—the shape of a goose egg. The light green sweater I wore reflected my skin favorably. Standing 5'4", I am the tallest woman in my family, although I am petite and exquisite like the rest. My shoulder-length black wavy hair got a little messy from walking outside in the blowing wind. I combed it in place with my fingers.

I looked down at the test. Only one pink line but the urine slowly moved to the right of the test window like waves pushing the shore, leaving behind wet marks on the sand. I took a deep breath, glanced at my watch, and then looked up again. In the mirror, my eyes squinted, my mouth closed tight and stretched to form a straight line.

Joe and I went through a rough time after 9/11. The small startup company he'd worked for closed its door shortly after the attack because it ran out of venture capital and was unable to secure new funding. Joe was out of a job for a year and a half, working tirelessly to start a business of his own. Many ideas were on the table, and a few were tried, but one by one they'd led to a dead end. More than a year later the stress was mounting. Earlier this year, things took a bad turn. My job was at risk. Joe started networking to get back to Argonne, the research lab he had left as a physicist during the economic boom in the late 90s. His effort paid off. They offered him a fabulous job, and they also rewrote the job description and title to match his experience and pay range.

Everything definitely changed post 9/11. Any previously perceived sense of security was non-existent. The economy was struggling to stay afloat. I sometimes worried about the future for our children. What kind of world are they going to live in?

There was another hidden concern always at the back of my mind. Joe's family has a history of lung cancer. His father died of it at the age of sixty-four. His oldest sister died when she was only forty-seven. When Jane and Michelle were only four and two, a routine x-ray screening showed a dark spot on Joe's lung. I found out by accident because Joe didn't want to worry me and thus didn't mention it. I couldn't sleep at all that night. I sobbed and went through all sorts of scenarios in my head. I wondered how I was going to raise two little girls on my own. Even though I was the one who took care of the intricate details of their lives, Joe was always there for us. He was a doting father, and he adored our daughters. We had each other's back, and the two of us made a great team. I needed him. I wasn't complete without him. It turned out that the spot was not cancerous. It was two crisscrossed veins going in different directions. It was a huge relief, and from that day on, I learned never to take life for granted. I would live every day as if it were a gift. This new insight strengthened our relationship and appreciation for life.

I looked down again and now there were two pink lines in the test window. I lifted up the test with my right hand, leaned on the counter with my right arm, and held it in front of my eyes. No doubt there were two lines. I knew what that meant. I felt a little dizzy, my heart pounding. I started to pace back and forth in the bathroom.

> *My settled life is going to change completely. Joe is forty-three and I am thirty-six. We're not old but not young. Are we ready for baby bottles and diapers again? And those long sleepless nights when the continuous cough of a sick child agonized me as I her and tried to soothe her but couldn't.*

Then I remembered how happy I was when I was pregnant—both times. Oh, the soft skin of a baby's face rubbing mine was just heavenly. Those little hands held so tightly to my finger. And the giggles of a baby simply filled the house with joy and happiness. And I absolutely loved the smell of babies!

"Yes. Of course, I'm ready to be a mommy again! I'm not going to let fear get in the way." I declared to my reflection in the mirror. *But how is Joe going to feel about this?* I was pretty sure I already knew the answer.

I stood at the door of the study, looking in. The walls were covered by light blue and brown pinstripe wallpaper. There was creamy white carpet on the floor. The computer desk was made of cherry with a matching credenza behind it. They gave our ordinary study an expensive look. Two black office chairs were in front of the desk facing Joe. Books, documents, multiple pen and pencil holders, bins, cups, and bottles that contained different vitamins and Joe's allergy medicines occupied the surface of the desk. It was a mess. Surprisingly Joe was able to find his things on this desk. Joe had an organizational system that only Joe could understand. There was a black-and-white picture of Jane and

Michelle on the wall. Next to it was a family photo taken at a studio in Shanghai three years ago. The photo shoot took nearly the entire day, and Joe had fallen asleep while they'd taken the shots of the girls and me. Joe stared at the monitor before him, eyebrows pinched together, chin rested on his right hand. He was in his own world. A world that was about to change.

"What are you thinking?" I asked, walking over and gently pressing down the black hair atop his head. Joe was already in his forties, but he looked at least ten years younger. And while he added weight in his belly area, he lost it on his head. What remained was thin and soft and liked to stick out. Now that I was close, I noticed just how good he smelled, fresh from the shower.

"Nothing much. Just reading some news." He moved his eyes from the monitor to me. His eyes sparkled.

"I have some news for you that will change your life forever."

"What is it? Tell me, tell me." He was like a little boy begging for candy.

I sat on his lap, my arms wrapped around his neck. "Do you love Jane and Michelle?"

"Oh, of course, I do. I love them very much, and I love you even more." He moved his hands up and down my back. His touch was gentle, soft, and soothing.

"Well. How do you feel about having another baby?"

"That will be wonderful. I will love it!"

"I know you want a boy, a mini-Joe. Admit it!"

"No, that is not true." He paused between every word and then continued slowly. "Another adorable mini-Linda will be just fine with me."

I didn't quite believe him, but it felt good to hear him say that. "I'm pregnant."

"You're kidding! Hooow? When?"

"Don't act so innocent. You were right there with me." I burst into laughter.

"Holy-moly, I'm going to be Daddy again. I love you, I love you, I love you!"

"But aren't we too old to have a baby? Jane is already ten and Michelle eight. We'll have to start all over again."

"Well, it's not too late. This is actually the perfect time to have a baby … and let me tell you why." He paused again, cleared his throat, as he often did. This time he was coming up with a list of reasons.

During the silence, I jumped in, expressing my concern, "What if you die on me? I will have to raise this baby all by myself."

"Well, if that ever happened … you may have a little man in the house helping you out."

"So you really want this baby?" I wanted confirmation.

"Yes. One hundred percent sure. You?"

"OK, then. Let us have another baby!"

\*

The first appointment I could get with Dr. Chang was mid-December. Her office was at the corner on the first floor of a three-story building. There were about a dozen chairs with thick blue back cushions lining two walls. A brown end table stood at the corner where the chairs met. The receptionists sat behind a glass window and there were two doors on either side of the window. Every once in awhile, a nurse would pop out behind one of the doors and call out someone's name. The strong smell of hand sanitizer was in the air.

Dr. Chang was in her early forties with a round face, short dyed brownish hair, slanted eyes, and smooth, shiny skin. Her smile was genuine, and she spoke hesitantly with a stutter. She speaks perfect English and good Mandarin. I liked the fact that she was bilingual because I didn't know all the medical terms in English. Unlike me, who came to the U.S. after college, she'd come when she was a toddler. After performing an internal examination, she confirmed that the pregnancy was progressing along nicely and the baby was bigger than what it was supposed to be at seven weeks.

My first two pregnancies were trouble-free, and I kind of expected this one to be good too. So I asked her the question that had been on my mind for the last few weeks. "Dr. Chang, we made plans to visit family and relatives in China this Christmas. Do you see any risk in my taking the trip?"

"No, I don't really see why you can't go, but as a precaution, let me prescribe an ultrasound just to make sure everything is OK."

She'd said what I'd wanted to hear. Three days later, I dashed into the medical center like someone was chasing me. I was instructed to drink thirty-two ounces of water before I left home, and by now I could barely hold it. I shifted in my chair, fidgeting. I simply can't hold water. I could hardly do it when I was pregnant with Jane and Michelle. Now that I was older, it was almost impossible. I'm convinced that I either have a very small bladder or the muscles that control my bladder are very weak. A few more seconds passed, and the choice became as clear as the water I drank. I ran for the bathroom. Just then my name was called. "I'll be right back!" I shouted. As I was sitting on the toilet, feeling a tremendous sense of relief, someone from the other side of the door said, "Try to hold back some."

I was quickly led into a little ultrasound room. There was a bed on the side next to the door, an ultrasound machine by the bed, a chair in front of the monitor, and a simple painting with just a few colored lines on the white wall. A woman in a light blue scrub top and matching pants walked in. She was big, with curly brunet hair, pale skin, and double chins.

"You just went to the bathroom and emptied your bladder?" She didn't look pleased.

"Sorry, I couldn't hold anymore."

Without even looking at me, she continued, "How far along are you pregnant?"

"Seven or eight weeks, I think."

"Okay. Let's try to find a heartbeat."

She pulled the chair out, slowly sat down, and got to work. There was dead silence in the room for a few minutes. The woman stared at the monitor with a confused look on her face. The look on her face unsettled me. Meanwhile the scanner frantically poked around my belly.

Finally, "I'm afraid there's no baby in your uterus." She declared.

"What? That's not possible!" *What a cruel joke! She didn't have to do that just because I went to the bathroom.*

"Maybe you're not as far along as you think. I recommend you go to Hinsdale Hospital today since they have newer and better equipment. We'll call your doctor to make the arrangement." She actually smiled and was much nicer to me.

It was already late afternoon, and I was annoyed. *I didn't plan for this. I don't have time to go to the hospital. We're leaving for China early tomorrow morning, and I still have a lot of packing to do.*

Then a voice came from above, "But do you want to find out if there is a problem with the baby?"

That voice always had a special effect on me. God and I had a personal way of communicating with each other. Looking up, I answered, "Yes, I do. I guess I'll go to the hospital and get this straightened out."

I called Joe. "Daddy, there may be a problem with my pregnancy. They can't find the baby. They want me to go to the Hinsdale for a recheck." I said quickly, my voice trembling a bit.

"I'll go with you."

As I was driving home, my mind was bombarded with all sorts of questions. *What did she mean by there "was no baby" in my uterus? Where is the baby? What can be wrong? Oh God, please give us a healthy baby just like you did with my first two pregnancies.*

After dinner, Joe and I got into the car for the hospital. I didn't bother to drink any water. There was no point. I wouldn't be able to hold it through the forty-minute car ride. Neither of us spoke at first.

"What could be wrong with the baby?" I finally broke the silence.

"Probably nothing. The baby might be smaller than seven weeks like the technician said."

"But Dr. Chang thought it was bigger."

"We'll find out soon. Don't worry, baby. Everything will be fine." He reached out for my hand and held it.

I turned to look at him. His eyes were fixed on the road. He was quieter than usual. The jolly Christmas music on the radio didn't help.

I looked out of the window, gazing far into the distance. Only nine more days to Christmas! The trees in the street were all lit up as cars zoomed by in a hurry to get places. Tomorrow morning I should be on the plane that would take me back to Shanghai, the place that held mixed childhood memories. I knew our families were looking forward to seeing us. I hadn't been back since Grandma passed away three years ago. Grandma had raised me.

Oh, how I had missed her! For a long time, I had no desire to return to Shanghai. I was not ready to face my mother again yet, but three years was a long time. Eventually I got excited about seeing the rest of my family, my uncles, my sister, my cousins, and nephews. Originally we planned to go during the summer when Jane and Michelle were out of school. The spread of SARS in Asia forced us to put it on hold. So this was a trip long overdue. On top of that we had told them about the baby. It was excitement all around!

My cell phone rang. It was my pastor from Living Water Church. I had served a number of terms on the board of deacons, and Rev. Zhong and I had worked on a few important church projects together. He was on his way to our church's weekly prayer meeting. I briefed him on the situation and asked everyone to pray for us.

After what seemed like a very long ride, we arrived at the hospital parking lot. It was frigidly cold outside. I could see my own breath. A thin layer of solid gray ice covered parts of the parking lot. Christmas lights glittered on trees and bushes under a blanket of snow. *It has to be difficult to spend Christmas in a hospital no matter how Christmassy it looks.* Joe came to my side; hand-in-hand we walked into the building.

This time without waiting, we were led into a cozy-looking ultrasound room with matching auburn floral wallpaper and carpet. A picture of a cuddly teddy bear in a gold frame hung on the wall. There was nobody in the waiting area. I was their last appointment for the day. A young technician with red hair stepped in. "Let's try to find that baby." As she searched for the embryo, I fixed my eyes on her face: the same puzzled look. My heart sank. After a few more minutes of silence, she went outside of the room.

"I have got your doctor on the phone." The technician handed me the phone when she finally came back.

"Hello?" I cautiously talked into the receiver.

"Hello, this is Dr. Simon. I'm on call tonight. We need to see you in the office tomorrow morning."

"No! I can't be in your office tomorrow morning. I'll be on a plane."

"There may be serious problems with your pregnancy. We need to check it out. You shouldn't go on a plane."

"But you don't understand, doctor! It's almost Christmas. Our families in China are waiting for us. I have to go. I'll see a doctor in Shanghai."

"If this is a tubal pregnancy and your tube bursts on the plane, you are not going to make it."

It had been such a long, agonizing day. The doctor's indifferent voice annoyed me. I was about to burst into tears. I handed the phone to Joe. "This doctor doesn't make any sense. You talk to him."

"Hello, doctor. Yes, yes, I understand. But a few of my friends are doctors working in the hospitals with world-class facilities in Shanghai. I'll take her to see them as soon as we get there."

He then paused and listened attentively for a few minutes. "Okay. Yes, yes. We'll see Dr. Chang in the office tomorrow morning. Bye."

I looked at him in disbelief. "What did he say that changed your mind?"

"He said he couldn't stop us from going. But if your tube bursts on the plane, it will be deadly. We are not going."

It was as if I was on a train that had to make a hasty and unexpected stop. But it did stop. *Alright! If both the doctor and my husband think we shouldn't go, we aren't going. Period. OK, God. I heard you. But what's next?*

When we got home it was almost ten o'clock. I could hear Jane and Michelle talking loudly and laughing in their room. They still shared the same bedroom even though they could have their own. The room had two identical white twin beds with scalloped headboards, patterned, multi-colored Nautica comforters, and nightstands. A picture of a colorful flower in a white frame hung above each bed.

The girls had been told there were a lot of presents waiting for them at their auntie's home in Shanghai. On top of that, they got to skip school for a week. We had to tell them, there was no other way. Joe and I looked at each other. He was to deliver the devastating news. I looked away.

Joe sat on Jane's bed, cleared his throat loudly. "Girls, it looks like there may be a problem with the baby. The doctor wants to see mommy tomorrow morning. Well, well, which means, it means …. You know what it means, right?"

"What does it mean, Daddy?" Michelle stared at Joe from her bed wide-eyed. "Well, it means we won't be able to go to Shanghai."

"Nooooo! I told everyone we were going away. We are all packed. We have to go, we have to, Daddy!" Jane was getting upset.

The next thing I knew, wailing and screaming filled the room. I wanted to cry too, but I knew that wouldn't help.

"Jane, Michelle, listen." I fought to hold back my tears and reached out for their hands. "We can always go to China another time. We just can't leave tomorrow."

"What about our presents?" Michelle sobbed.

"Da Ma Ma (Joe's sister) will save them for you. You can open them when we go later."

"What's wrong with the baby?" Michelle asked.

"Well, they can't find the baby in my tummy."

"Does that mean the baby is dead?" Jane had hoped for a little brother.

"I just don't know."

\*

All of us piled into the car early next morning. Instead of heading to the airport, we drove to the doctor's office. Jane and Michelle were too upset to go to school. They had told all their friends that they were going away for the holidays. The nurse took us to Dr. Chang's office. She asked me to sit on the exam table, and Joe and the girls on the chairs.

Doctor Chang walked in with my ultrasound reports in her hand, "Linda, do you feel any abdominal pain?" She asked while acknowledging everyone in the room.

I experienced some abdominal pain very early in the pregnancy, but it went away quickly and so I didn't think much of it.

"No," I replied.

"There could only be three possibilities," her stutter seemed more obvious today and she talked more slowly. "One, you had a miscarriage without knowing it. That's the best scenario. Two, this is a molar pregnancy, meaning the tissue that normally becomes a fetus instead becomes an abnormal growth in your uterus. Looking at the ultra-sound images, I can see a dark shade in your uterus, which could be the molar growth. Three, this is a tubal pregnancy. Tubal pregnancy occurs when the embryo gets stuck in your tube. Since you haven't experienced any abdominal pain, it's unlikely to be that. We'll have to do blood work to find out. But call us immediately if you experience any abdominal pain, OK?"

I quickly assessed each scenario. *How could I have a miscarriage without knowing it? Not possible. Molar pregnancy? That sounds nasty. Joe's sister had a molar pregnancy many years ago and she had to go through chemo and lost all her hair. Any abnormal growth is not good, that I know. Can this be a tubal pregnancy? As the embryo grows in the tube, there should be tension and pain. Why haven't I felt any pain?*

Dr. Chang explained further that it would take two blood tests to figure out what type of pregnancy mine was. The first one would be taken today and then the same test would be repeated 48 hours later, which meant we would have the answer some time Saturday morning. At the time it sounded like a good plan. In three days, we'd get to the bottom of this, and the doctors would know how to handle this abnormal pregnancy.

I should have asked what they would do if it turned out to be molar or tubal, but I didn't. For some reason Joe, who normally likes to have answers for everything, didn't either. Everything happened like a whirlwind, which put us in a state of shock.

After the blood test, we went to a nearby Japanese-Korean restaurant for lunch. Nothing tasted good that day. Even Jane and Michelle who loved sushi and eating out barely touched their food. They sulked. I felt thick in the head, struggling to make sense of all that was happening.

The phone rang non-stop after we got home. Loving and concerning church brothers and sisters were calling to find out how I was doing. "I am OK. But it doesn't look like we are going to have a baby. We'll find out on Saturday what kind of pregnancy this is after two blood tests. I'll be fine, really." After repeating the same lines over and over again, I was almost convinced that everything would indeed be fine.

Suddenly my life was on a holding pattern, and I had all this free time on hand which felt strange. I knew I would go crazy sitting around waiting for the blood results. Looking around, I decided that the house needed a thorough cleaning. I rolled up my sleeves and got to work. I mopped, vacuumed, scrubbed, and even went under the beds to get rid of the dust bunnies. The phone kept on ringing. Joe would pick it up, and people would ask to talk to me. The thickness in my head was dissipating. I was able to laugh on the phone, telling friends not to worry about me, "I'll be just fine."

I went back for the second blood test on Friday as I was instructed. We were moving closer to getting the answer.

Living Water Church was going to have its annual Christmas program on Friday evening. Joe and I decided to go. It would keep our mind off things. Plus it would be good to see the brothers and sisters and let everyone know that we were doing well under the circumstances. Joe and I attracted a small crowd as soon as we got into the church building. Many people expressed concern, best wishes, and would continue to pray for us. As we made our way to the auditorium talking to everyone along the path, our choir conductor ran towards me. I told her it could be molar or tubal. She looked at me ever so seriously and said, "I used to work in a hospital in China. When a pregnant woman came to the hospital with a ruptured tube, the doctor would cut her open immediately and operate on her. It's a life and death situation." Her eyes popped out and her smile froze. It scared me. For the first time since all this happened, I was afraid, afraid of what was going to happen to me.

The lights dimmed. Christmas music filled every corner of the auditorium. I sat down, put my head on Joe's shoulder and whispered, "I am scared." He wrapped his arm around my shoulder and kissed me on the cheek, this time without saying anything.

The theater-style auditorium has about 500 creamy fabric seats. We occupied almost half of the first floor. The balcony was nearly empty. It was artistically decorated for the holiday season. Two brightly lit Christmas trees stood tall in front of the stage on both sides. A black grand piano sat gracefully on the left side of the stage, and on the other side, a drum set behind a five-panel drum shield. Sparkling garlands ran along the half walls across the auditorium. The sound system was top-notch. Cylindrical lighting fixtures hung low from the ceiling. This gorgeous facility belongs to a local American church. We'd rented it for our Christmas program. Living Water Church didn't have its own church building yet. Our Sunday service was held in the gym of a junior high school.

The Christmas program consisted of performances by the choir, each Bible study group, and concluded by a short Christmas message from the pastor. It was loosely put together but nevertheless fun to watch. Throughout the program, my mind jumped around, not able to focus. Joe and I held hands. He turned and smiled at me from time to time.

After the program, we waved goodbye to everyone, promising we'd keep them posted on the situation. It was after 10:30 p.m. when we got home. Jane and Michelle changed into their pajamas and settled for bed. I went to their room as usual, tucked them in and kissed them good night. I was happy that another long day was about to pass. There would be answers in the morning. I didn't want to think about what was going to happen. No, not yet. I'd worry about that tomorrow.

Things almost never happen according to plan. I was about to get the answer I'd been waiting for the last three days before the new day arrived. It was not the answer anyone had expected. It hit me like a bullet.

*

"Daddy, come!" I screamed frantically.

Joe ran into the bathroom where I'd been brushing my teeth. I was rolling on the floor, clenching my stomach.

"What's happening, baby?" He panted.

" It feels like I am going to have a massive diarrhea …"

Joe held me up to get to the toilet. I sat down and looked into the toilet bowl, but there was no blood, nothing.

"I'm calling the doctor," Joe cried.

Doctor Simon was on call again that night. He wanted to talk to me.

"Linda, what's going on?"

"I am experiencing terrible abdominal pain. I can barely move."

"On the scale on one to ten, ten being the worst, how bad is the pain?"

"Eleven," I groaned. My voice got weaker within just the last few minutes.

"Which hospital is the closest to you?"

"Edward."

"I'll see you there." He hung up the phone.

With Joe's help, I put on my coat and boots. He went to Jane and Michelle's room to get them out of bed.

"Girls, we have to go to the hospital right away. Mommy is having an emergency."

Jane and Michelle were already asleep but they were fully aware of the situation and jumped out of bed and got ready in lightening speed.

Edward hospital was only five minutes away. We figured it would be quicker to get there on our own instead of calling the ambulance. This turned out to be a bad decision that almost cost me my life.

When we got into the emergency building, no hospital staff was in sight. There were a few wheel chairs by the door. I sat on one of them and Joe pushed me to the registration area. Two patients were ahead of me. He approached the receptionist sitting behind the glass window and said, "My wife may have a tubal pregnancy, and she is in great pain."

"Take a seat. We'll get to her as soon as we can." She replied, only briefly looking up from the paperwork she was working on.

Joe came back to me. "Baby, we'll have to wait. They'll take care of you shortly."

"I don't think I can hold on much longer." I looked at him desperately and mouthed the words "Help me, please!"

Joe went back to the window but was again told to wait. Fifteen minutes later, a nurse came by and requested information from me such as my name, address, insurance, and the reason for the visit.

Joe pleaded with her, "She really needs help now! Can you do something please?"

"There are two people in front her. We are working as fast as we possibly can." She looked at me and walked away.

I had no reason to come to the Edward emergency room before. It blew my mind that seeing the dire condition I was in, the nurse just walked away. Was I low priority because I didn't arrive in an ambulance? It didn't make any sense. Here I was barely hanging on to life, but nobody in this hospital cared!

I turned to Joe and then to Jane and Michelle, "Please pray for me."

The four of us bowed our heads, held hands, and Joe prayed, "Heavenly Father, please save my wife's life. Keep her safe. Give us the wisdom to know what to do. Thank you Lord! In Jesus' name. Amen."

I opened my eyes and turned to Joe again. "Daddy, please take me to the Hinsdale hospital."

I only went to Hinsdale a few times for tests and examinations. But I liked the atmosphere there, particularly the friendly staff members.

"But it's forty minutes away."

"Take me, please."

"Okay!"

He pushed me towards the door with Jane and Michelle in tow. We waited while Joe went to the parking lot to get the car. Nobody was at the entrance area, so we left without being noticed. When our white Ford Windstar pulled up, I abandoned the wheel chair and crawled into the car with Jane and Michelle's help.

Joe tried to make every traffic light to get to Hinsdale in record time. I collapsed in the front passenger seat. It felt like I was shot in the stomach only there was no blood. My face turned completely pale, and I was perspiring to the point of passing out. I started to wonder if it was a good idea to give up my spot at Edward. I was uncertain if I was going to make it to Hinsdale alive. Then a song came to mind, a familiar song we sang often during Sunday worship and Bible study gatherings. A Chinese countryside girl who only had elementary school education wrote it. As a matter of fact, she had written close to a thousand worship songs that were very popular among the Chinese Christian community. I hummed it silently.

*Lord, you are my most intimate friend, my dearest companion.*

*My heart desires you every day, longing to be with you.*

*Every step I take in my life, every stop I make, your hand holds mine, keeping me to your side.*

*What else do I need when I have you?*

*My heart is tied to yours.*

*Your love is so deep and wide that I am in awe.*

*Lord, you are my most intimate friend, my dearest companion.*

*My heart desires you every day, longing to be with you.*

*Every step I take in my life, every stop I make, your hand holds mine, keeping me to your side.*

*Direct me the path I should follow so that I won't slide down the valley of death.*

*I have determined to follow you, for the rest of my life.*

I didn't know how many times I sang the song in my head. Occasionally, I dug my fingers in my thigh, clenched my teeth and hunched over to battle the waves of the excruciating pain.

Eventually, we got on the little wooden bridge that only one car could pass at a time. The hospital was just on the other side. Joe turned off the engine outside the emergency room and helped me get out of the car. As soon as we entered the building through the automatic door, he yelled, "My wife's tube ruptured. Someone help her now!" I moved forward slowly holding his arm with my torso bent ninety degrees. A male nurse ran to me with an empty wheel chair. After I got settled in the chair, he pushed me directly to an open room.

In the emergency room, an IV needle was immediately inserted into the vein on the back of my hand. The ultrasound revealed severe internal bleeding. The room was now buzzing, and I heard people running and yelling "Ectopic! Ectopic!"

I uttered an anguished moaning when the catheter was put in. This must be the life-and-death situation my choir conductor was talking about.

Someone got my doctor's phone number from Joe and quickly got on the phone to call him. I also heard Joe telling someone about my pregnancy and what we had gone through in the last few days. He was then asked to fill out a stack of forms. Joe sat down next to Jane and Michelle who were huddling at the corner, watching everything that was going on with horror and curiosity.

"Is mommy going to die?" Michelle whispered.

"No, Mommy is not going to die. She will be OK. Don't you worry about it, OK, baby?"

"I was at the Edward hospital looking for her, and they told me she wasn't there anymore. She should have stayed there and waited for me." Doctor Simon walked into the room complaining noisily. I followed the sound and took a good look at him. This was the first time I had ever met him in person. He wore thick, black-rimmed eyeglasses. His hair was uncombed like he'd just gotten out of bed. He was sort of heavy, and his belly stuck out. His lab coat could use a wash. Dr. Simon looked sloppy. He also took a long, hard look at me. When he saw the miserable state I was in, he stopped whining and got to work immediately.

Dr. Simon ordered blood tests in preparation for the blood transfusion. Meanwhile, he handed me a couple of forms. "By signing these, you allow me to do whatever it takes to save your life. If necessary, I may have to take out your uterus or whatever it takes." He was not going to leave anything to my imagination. I hadn't decided if I could trust him, but I had no choice. After all, I knew who ultimately held my destiny. I signed the forms and handed them back to him.

I was to be moved to the operating room for surgery. Joe and the girls came to my side. Joe bent over me to gently caress my face. His gaze was deep, full of tenderness, love, and maybe a little fear. Jane and Michelle looked tired, unsure, and scared. I pressed my hand on each of theirs and mouthed, "I love you," before they took me out of the room.

\*

"Her blood pressure is getting dangerously low. She's not going to hang on much longer. Hurry up! Let's get her into the operation room quick!" The doctor urgently hustled the nurses who were trying to get me ready for surgery.

"We're waiting for blood from the blood bank," replied one of the nurses.

I glanced at the monitor. The green line that tracked my blood pressure had a steep drop and was flattening out. The pain was becoming unbearable. It felt like there was an earthquake inside me. Every bone was cracking and every muscle stretched beyond its limit. *Is this it for me? Am I going to die tonight? I didn't get a chance to say good-bye to my beloved Joe and Jane and Michelle who mean everything to me. My babies are going to grow up without their mommy.* Tears welled up in my eyes and rolled down my cheeks. *I am not afraid of dying. But if I have a choice in this matter, God, I choose to live. I want to grow old with Joe. I want to see my girls grow up.*

"Linda, I need you to stay awake. Don't fall asleep. Stay with me." This was my doctor's voice. "How old are you, Linda?" He tried again to keep me awake.

"Thirrrty-ssssixx," I mumbled.

Everything—the nurses hovering over me, the illuminating lamps, the machine with the green line, and the doctor standing next to me started to blur. *If I die today, at least the pain will stop. I will be in heaven with God. It will be hard for my family, but everything will be OK. Joe will take care of the girls. They will figure out a way to move on without me.* I drifted away, fading into the unconsciousness.

\*

"Linda, wake up. It is time to wake up, Linda."

I slowly opened my eyes. *Where am I? Am I in heaven? Are the angels calling me to come in?* I tried to move my legs but was immediately reminded of the pain my earthly body was experiencing.

*I can't be in heaven because there's no pain, either physical or emotional, in heaven. I didn't die. I'm alive!* As the room slowly came into focus, I saw a middle-aged woman with an angelic voice and short blond hair leaning over me, a gentle smile on her face. She wore an ocean-blue cotton smock with brown teddy bears all over it. The blue color gave me a sense of serenity. The teddy bears welcomed me back with open arms and chubby legs. I still remember the nurse's sweet comforting voice, the voice that awakened me from a deep sleep and brought me back to this world.

It was still dark, although the morning light tried to break through. The atmosphere was extraordinarily quiet and tranquil. One could hear a pin drop. I found myself lying on a hospital bed with needles stuck in both my arms and machines hooked to my body. The room looked familiar. It was big but felt empty. There were a few metal cabinets by the wall and some medical instruments scattered around. The smell of bleach soaked the air.

"I am very cold," I murmured to the nurse in a faint voice that could barely be heard.

"I can do something about that." She opened one of the cabinets and quickly took out a few more blankets and wrapped me up in them.

"What time is it?" I asked.

"It's seven a.m. Your surgery lasted more than five hours. Now you're in the recovery room."

The kind nurse handed me a small rubber balloon and said, "If you feel pain, just squeeze this."

Her hands felt soft and warm. She folded my swollen fingers around the rubber balloon as if she was sure I would need it soon. All of a sudden I recalled that last night, my husband and daughters accompanied me to the Hinsdale Hospital emergency room.

"Where is my husband?" I asked anxiously. They must have had been so worried about me. I could still see the panic on Jane and Michelle's innocent faces in the emergency room amidst all of the chaos and commotion. In the twenty years I had known Joe, he had never come as close to losing it as yesterday. His gaze was so solemn as if he were going to lose something essential to his life.

"He's in the waiting room. He and your daughters have been there all night. We'll call him and tell him you're awake and on your way to your room."

As I lay on the bed being pushed to my ward, I looked up and saw the nurse's ocean-blue uniform like a backdrop above my head. The experience of the last three weeks was like sailing in the calm sea on a sunny day and suddenly being thrown into a fierce storm and forced to fight for my life. Life has a strange way of changing its course unexpectedly. My bed turned into a long hallway with a window at the very end. As we approached the window, I was amazed to see the bright sunlight finally shining through.

*I am rescued. I made it through the shipwreck, barely in one piece, but I survived! It sure is good to be back. Thank you God! I will love and enjoy my family everyday and I am going to serve you for the rest of my life!*

I gave the little balloon a hard squeeze.

\*

"Mommy, Mommy!" I heard Jane and Michelle's running feet when my bed was about to make a turn into my ward.

Suddenly the running stopped. Jane and Michelle stood a few feet from me and had the identical astonished look on their faces. "Mommy's eyes are open. That means she is alive." Jane whispered to Michelle, and Michelle nodded.

They were still in their little pajamas, their long hair rather messy. I smiled at them and moved my fingers to indicate that it would be OK to come closer. And they did.

"Mommy, you look so pale … like a ghost." Michelle stared at me.

"Do those needles hurt?" Jane pointed at my arms.

I smiled again and shook my head.

Joe gave me a kiss on the forehead and whispered in my ear, "Welcome back, baby! We missed you!"

"Glad to be back," I whispered.

"You know what, girls? I'm going to take you home. You're going to stay with Grace and Joy's family for a few days until mommy gets out of the hospital."

"Sleepover, yeeaahh!" they cheered.

"Mommy, when are you going home?"

"Soon, baby, real soon," I mumbled. I wanted to be home for Christmas.

It was a small and cozy hospital room with the same carpet and wallpaper as the ultrasound room. My bed was parked in the middle of the room against the wall, a bathroom to my left, a recliner close to the door and a couple of chairs for visitors.

When Joe came back, he brought me the stuff I would need in the hospital: toothbrush, toothpaste, pajamas, comb, dental floss. I was so tired and drugged that I slept for the better part of the day, though the nurses who came in to check my temperature, blood pressure, and replenish the IV medications woke me up frequently.

Dr. Simon stopped by too. He looked more civilized today with his face shaved, hair combed, and a big smile on his face.

"I still can't believe that you guys left Edward Hospital like that. You took a big risk."

"Nobody there was going to take care of her. We did the right thing by leaving. Don't you think, doc?" Joe replied matter-of-factly.

"You must have good connections up there." Dr. Simon pointed to the ceiling and then turned to me.

I smiled and nodded. I started to like this doctor.

He told Joe after the operation that I had lost almost a gallon of blood. The danger of kidney failure was imminent. He thought I was lucky to be alive.

Dr. Simon lifted the cover and my blue cotton hospital gown to check my abdomen. I had a hole on the right side of my belly with a dangling balloon sticking out to drain the remaining blood. My legs were wrapped with Rite-aid compression stockings that squeezed steadily to prevent blood clot. The catheter was still in so I didn't have to get up to go to the bathroom.

"I made three small abdominal incisions to remove the ectopic growth in the ruptured fallopian tube, and then I tied that tube. It took a couple of hours to drain all that blood, a whole gallon of it, whew!" He emphasized that the incisions were very small and therefore I should still be able to wear bikinis.

I chuckled to myself. Wearing a bikini was the last thing on my mind. The truth was that like most Asian women of my age, I had never worn bikinis in my life. But I appreciated the fact the Dr. Simon took that into consideration when he performed the surgery.

Dr. Simon called every morning to see how I was doing and paid a visit usually in the afternoon. He turned out to be a great doctor, highly skilled and deeply caring even though I still thought his white lab coat could use a wash.

On his second visit, Dr. Simon ordered to have the catheter taken out and encouraged me to get up, walk around, and eat to rebuild the red blood cells. The rubbery and overcooked hospital food was not enticing at all, and Joe ate most of it. I took the Jell-O cubes and orange juice.

Following Dr. Simon's advice, I tried to get out of bed and move around, but my physical condition was much worse than expected. The entire room spun around, moving stars popping everywhere in front my eyes, and I was completely out of breath. I laid down slowly without my feet even touching the floor.

With the catheter gone, I had to get up almost every hour to go to the bathroom. It was about a dozen steps away, but getting there turned out to be a chore. First Joe had to unplug the devices I was hooked to, help me sit up on my bed, give me a few minutes to balance myself and catch my breath, and then support me to stand up slowly. The IV stand had to walk with me. I would take a few breaks along the way. The first time I reached the bathroom and saw myself in the mirror above the sink, I got startled. No wonder Michelle took a step back when she saw me. I looked gaunt and totally pale. My hair tangled in a wild mess and my eyes stood out even bigger against my thinning face. I was like one of those injured ghostly figures in the Chinese Kung Fu movie.

My hourly trip to the bathroom became my daily exercises. I also slept less because of that. Joe rested whenever he could on the recliner. When I was awake, he would pull a chair to sit by the bed and tell me about the current news, events, and jokes he had read. When he ran out of those, he started telling me stories of all sorts. Joe was an interesting storyteller. He added lots of details to the material, and he could make the story go on and on. I usually fell asleep way before he got the end of it.

I stayed in the hospital four nights. They turned out to be some of the happiest days in my life. I was in a state of contradiction between body and mind. My body was going through a painful healing process. I was dependent on morphine to reduce the pain, and Joe to help me perform the simplest daily tasks. But my soul was at peace. I was content and happy inside. I knew God was right there with me. I could touch and feel him. He was that close! Joe's stories told in his soothing voice were like the warm breeze of early spring and running water in a little brook. I was soaked in love. Pain and loss lose its sting in the face of perfect love!

On Sunday afternoon, a dozen brothers and sisters, including Pastor Zhong and his wife, came to see me after the service. They formed a circle around my bed and prayed for my recovery and healing. Then they asked how I was doing, what they could cook for me, when I could go home. Joe answered all their questions since I was instructed to rest and not talk too much. Dr. Simon arrived in the middle of the conversation and told everyone, "Steaks, she needs to eat a lot of steaks." Everyone laughed and left shortly after.

Dr. Simon wanted to release me on the third day of my stay at the hospital but couldn't because I became feverish and my red blood cell count was too low. Normal RBC level for women is between 4 and 5, and mine was 1.1. My body was not reproducing RBC as fast as he had hoped. So I was to be given antibiotics through IV to bring the fever down as well as another blood transfusion.

Two days before Christmas, my temperature went below 100°F and RBC went up to 1.9. I was well enough to go home!

Before starting the car, Joe winked at me and asked, "How was our little getaway?"

"The best!" I turned to him and smiled a happy smile.

*

Joe carried me upstairs to our bedroom like a groom would take his bride. I held onto him tight, afraid he might drop me. I felt dizzy, and his steps were wobbly. He must be exhausted from sleeping in the recliner for four nights, interrupted constantly by people coming in and out of the room. We'd been married for fifteen years. In some profound ways, it felt like we were going to start a brand new life together again.

After helping me get comfortable in the bed, Joe brought a boom box to the room and turned on the worship music. "Sometimes there are dark clouds, sometimes there are storms. I look up to Jesus because he knows it all. He is my Lord and I am his creature. I hide myself in his arms because he knows it all ..." I closed my eyes and was immersed in the beautiful lyrics of the song. *Yes, I am home!* I thought to myself.

I dozed off and had a dream. In my dream, I was looking all over the places for my baby. I ended up in my aunt's place in the center of downtown Shanghai where I grew up. I turned into the alley that led to house I used to live in. The two-story Shikumen-style townhouses looked identical, with each residence connected and arranged in straight alleys as longtangs. The tall, heavy brick wall in front of them distinguished the front doors. I went in through the back door. It immediately opened to a public kitchen shared by the six families who lived in the house. There were six gas stoves and two large concrete sinks. A thick layer of black grease and dirt covered the walls. Everything in the kitchen was oily. People were busy making dinner. The strong aroma of the heated cooking oil mixed with garlic and various other food filled the air. The concrete floor was damp and sticky. The three households on the first floor shared one restroom that only had a toilet in it and lots of junk piled on the side. The toilet was behind the sinks separated by a wall with a window. My aunt's room was at the end directly facing the back door. There were two rooms to the right on the opposite side of the bathroom occupied by two other families. On the left side next to the bathroom, a wooden staircase led to the second floor. Instead of going into my home, I went upstairs. There were two rooms facing the staircase, another one at the end on the left. The people on the second floor shared a bathroom next to the staircase. On the right, taking a few steps down was another much smaller room. To the right of that little room, a concrete staircase led up to the balcony where clothes were hung on bamboo poles to dry.

It was at the top of the stairs to the balcony I found my baby. It was a boy! He sat there with no visible support, wrapped in hospital blankets. The baby resembled a five-month old boy in my church who had big brown eyes, fair skin, red cheeks, and lots of black hair. He didn't smile or make any baby noises. He just looked at me while I looked at him. Then he disappeared. I began to weep and woke up.

Raw emotion overtook me. I had lost my baby. He never got a chance at life because he was stuck in my tube. He could have grown to be a healthy, handsome, and wonderful person. But I would never get to see it because it was not meant to be. Big tears rolled down my cheeks and wet the comforter. I sobbed with my shoulders heaving up and down.

I remembered Grandma's heartbreak of losing her first three children, all boys, before they reached their first birthday. She became severely depressed. She would get up in the middle of the night and hire a manually pulled two-wheel yellow carriage. The puller held onto the long handles extended from the bottom of the carriage and ran with the passenger sitting behind him. She would tell the guy to keep on going until she found her babies. Her anxiety attacks went away once she got pregnant again. The baby girl survived. Then she had my mother, and three more boys after that. In fear of losing another son, she dressed my oldest uncle as a girl until he reached school age. I saw a picture of him when he was about five. He wore his long hair in two braids and a Buddhist necklace around his neck. Uncle looked rather cute as a girl! Now I understood how hard it must have been for Grandma to endure such tragic losses.

When the raw emotion receded, it was replaced by a sense of gratefulness. I was grateful to be able to meet my baby face to face even if it was only for five seconds. He would always be my little angel! Peace restored, I wiped away my tears.

For the next few days, I stayed in bed recuperating. One morning I was awake when Joe took a shower. The running water sounded like music to my ears. I dreamed that one day I would be strong enough to stand in the shower and let the hot water rinse my hair and my whole body. How wonderful would that be!

Lots of brothers and sisters from Living Water dropped in with homemade soup or dishes. The holiday season further fueled the giving spirit. Chinese people are big on nutritious soup. For someone like me who had just lost a ton of blood, it was even more appropriate. On any given day, I could sample three or four different types of soup. The food just kept on coming. I wasn't eating much, and neither was Joe. Jane and Michelle preferred American food to Chinese. So Joe came up with a swapping strategy by insisting that people take something untouched back home if they wanted to leave food with us. That worked out well.

I didn't see any of the visitors except my best friend Lin. Joe led her upstairs to my room. Lin is about ten years older than I am. She is a professor at a private college. Lin dresses like a professor, usually in a turtleneck and a blazer. She also talks like one. She speaks with precision and conviction and her gestures help drive her point home. Lin loves God and is passionate about spreading the gospel. Her husband had quit his job as an IT professional to become a seminary student. Lin always made a point of showing appreciation every time I was in the middle of coordinating a heavy-lifting church ministry project. Her praise was specific and genuine and it made all the hard work seem worthwhile. She would say, "Linda, you handled that situation so gracefully! I know this is a tough job, but you made it look so effortless." She is precious, and I love her.

Lin came into the room and stood by my bed. She looked at me and smiled lovingly. I didn't look like the old Linda who moved swiftly with determination who could keep all the balls in the air and catch them one by one. Here I was lying in bed, weak and fragile. But both she and I knew that in a few more days I would get up and charge ahead. Lin took my hand and prayed for me. Her voice cracked a little in the middle of the prayer. I squeezed her hand.

I got a little stronger every day. Four days after coming home from the hospital, I managed to get up by myself and made my way downstairs for the first time by holding onto the rail of the stairs. The kitchen took my breath away. There were roses and festive flowers in different vases on the counter. Pots, plates, bowls and serving platters stacked on top of each other. I hoped Joe would remember to whom we should return them. But I knew he wouldn't. We would just have to take all of them to church and ask people to claim them.

The glass and aluminum containers glittered in the afternoon sunlight flooding in through the windows. Standing in the middle of my kitchen, I was overwhelmed by the tremendous love that poured on me in the past week. Over the years, the church had become my community, my support, and my family!

I finally took a shower the next morning before going to the follow-up appointment with Dr. Simon. It turned out to be a quick one because I got nauseated almost immediately. I got dressed, dried my hair, and put on some makeup. Although still pale and gaunt, I looked more alive especially with the help of the makeup.

Dr. Simon had a curious look on his face when he saw me in his office. "Wow! Look at what a difference a few days can make! You have got some color on your cheeks!" He took the stitches off my abdomen and sent me off for another blood test. He told Joe and me that I would have to take a blood test every week for the next few weeks to ensure my hormone went down and RBC count went up to the normal levels. "Eat lots of steaks to build up those red blood cells." He reminded me again.

I took six weeks off from work to get fully mended. It was a restful six weeks, lots of naps. On a sunny day, I would lie on the sofa in front of the living room bay window and read books. Sometimes Joe surprised me by coming home for lunch. I also worked with the vendor and got the church photo directory finalized and printed. It felt like a big accomplishment. Life was slowly going back to normal. I went for another follow-up appointment with Dr. Chang a month after the surgery. She thought my recovery was heading in the right direction.

As I got up to leave, she said something that took me by surprise. "You know, Linda, if you want another baby, it's technically possible. You still have a good tube, so it can be done."

*Another baby? But it'll be insane to try again! I already have two beautiful children. I am completely happy. No more babies.* I reasoned with myself. But there was a quiet yearning of wanting something even more only after losing it in the first place. "I—I don't know if I have the courage to go through it again." I replied.

"We can't do anything about courage, but if you ever decide to get pregnant again, we are here to help." She smiled.

# Anything for Love

A year and a half after we cancelled the trip to Shanghai due to my ectopic pregnancy, Joe, Jane, Michelle, and I landed at the Shanghai PuDong airport in the heat of the summer after a fourteen-hour direct flight. It had been five years since I last set my foot in Shanghai. The newly constructed airport was very modern and kept spic-and-span clean, unlike many Shanghai streets.

As we stepped out of the baggage claim area, I scanned the crowd waiting outside for familiar faces. I saw my uncle Mao Mao, my sister, and her husband. My sister waved to us enthusiastically. I waved back. We inched forward behind a long line of people and luggage carts. When we finally reached them, it was obvious that my sister was thrilled to see us again after five years.

"Wow! Jin, Meechelle, you are so big now! You were only this tall last time." My sister put her hand over her waist. This loud over-excited woman who they barely remembered took Jane and Michelle aback.

"How was your trip?" Uncle Mao Mao asked in a soft voice, smiling. He looked much older since most of his teeth were gone and he was as thin as a stick.

"Good! No problems at all," I answered.

The minute we walked outside to get in the taxi line, it was like stepping into a big oven. The temperature was well above 100°F under the scorching sun. The air was damp and stifling. There was no breeze whatsoever. With all the taxis queued in a long line, the smell of gasoline from the car exhaust system blasted the air. Oh, yeah, welcome to Shanghai!

When Joe, Jane, Michelle, and I got into our taxi, Jane said to me, "Mom, your sister is soooo weird."

"I know," I chuckled.

Shanghai looked familiar but strange at the same time. There were a lot more cars on the road. People drove recklessly, cutting off one another and cursing at each other. Skyscrapers and stacks of tall apartment buildings dominated the skyline. The taxi took us on the Yangpu Bridge. With a total length of 27,400 feet, it is one of the largest cable-stayed bridges in the world. Even on this magnificent bridge, we were going less than twenty miles an hour. The driver cussed the huge population in Shanghai that caused traffic jams everywhere. Once off the bridge, cars, bikers, and pedestrians flocked the road. Most people dressed stylishly and yet public spitting could still be witnessed frequently. Along the streets stood numerous contemporarily decorated stores and restaurants, but the sidewalks were covered by dirty water carelessly splashed out by the business owners. Shanghai was loud. People didn't talk, they yelled at each other. Cars honking, buses announcing stop names, elevated the noise level, street vendors crying out for customers, and bargaining conducted in roaring voices. Finally we arrived at Uncle Mao Mao's place, which Joe and I made a down payment for years ago when it was being constructed. At the time, we didn't have enough money to buy Grandma her own apartment. But I wanted to make a significant contribution to Grandma's new home with Uncle Mao Mao. The apartment was on the fourth floor of a six-story apartment building that was only six years old but looked dusty and stained with rust. Grandma lived here for less than a year before she passed away. She would have been waiting for me here by the entrance door if she knew I was coming home, but there was no sign of her this time. I was overcome by a sense of loss and sadness. We got our luggage upstairs and entered the apartment.

This was my second time to Mao Mao and Yanhua's home. It is a three-bedroom and two-bathroom unit with two living rooms. On a cooler day with the sliding doors to the balcony open, you can hear the cars on the street whooshing by and people chatting down below. The apartment was divided into two sections by a glass door with a wooden frame. Between the main door and the glass door are one of the two living rooms with an old sofa, a dining table, the kitchen, and a bathroom. The dining table was jammed with all sorts of stuff and was obviously not used for dining purposes anymore. Beyond the glass door, another living room with the gray leather sofas, coffee table, and a TV, the bedrooms, a second bathroom and the balcony. Uncle and Yanhua must have had thoroughly cleaned up the apartment prior to our arrival but a new layer of dust was starting to collect.

I went into Grandma's bedroom. It now had two twin beds for Jane and Michelle to sleep in during our two-week stay. "Hi, Grandma, I'm back!" I sat down on the bed close to the door, resting my chin on the tips of my fingers. Images of her flooded my mind.

Grandma was a very petite lady who was only 4'5" tall and weighed eighty pounds. At the age of eighty-nine, her hair was still grayish black. She combed it neatly back and twisted a bun on the back of her head. She often wore an apron over the blue tie-dye vest I bought her. Even though she was small, one shouldn't be fooled by her size: she was one tough lady.

The Cultural Revolution kicked into full gear the year I was born. My grandfather (my father's father) was a wealthy banker, a capitalist, the target of the Revolution. The government seized his fortune after he died. I never got to see the grandparents from my father's side. Grandfather passed away before the Revolution, barely escaping the harsh and cruel reality he would have had to otherwise face. Grandmother died of fear and anxiety when the environment was getting increasingly hostile and violent towards people of her class.

My father was sent to Yun Nan located in the far southwest of China to be reformed because of his family background. He didn't have the freedom to come and go as he wished and therefore he wasn't able to accompany my mother to Shanghai when she gave birth to me. Grandma was already raising my sister Yiwen before I came along. Yiwen was born in Yun Nan, premature with osteomalacia. My parents tried to keep her with them but gave up after a year. It was too hard to raise a baby with health issues especially when they had to move from place to place because of their assignments. So Grandma traveled a week one way by train and then by buses through the mountain areas, picked up Yiwen and brought her back to Shanghai. Even though Dad's family owned a whole Shikumen house, when I was born, the Red Guards occupied the house. My sister and I had no place to live.

Determined to put a roof over our heads, Grandma camped out with a toddler and an infant in one of the rooms in the house my father's family owned. Grandma was born poor, and she married someone of her class, so they had no reason to oppress her. But the Red Guards took away the burners to the gas stove in an effort to drive us out. Grandma persisted. With the help of family and friends, we stayed there day after day and managed to preserve a room in 930 Long Unit #4 that we could call our home.

I lived there for the first few years of my life. Other families started to move in, and eventually every room was occupied. But I had my little room on the second floor and I had Grandma. I was happy!

When I was three, Grandma's older daughter and her family moved into a Shikumen house two miles east of where we lived. Aunt asked Grandma to live with them and take care of her kids as well. So we moved and merged with Aunt's family. My happy life turned to be not so happy after that.

Aunt's family of five lived in a ten-by-fourteen square-foot single room. With the addition of Grandma, Grandpa, Yiwen, and I, the small space became awfully crowded. We had three beds, one for Grandma and me, one for Grandpa and Qiqi (my cousin), and a big bed for the three girls (my other two cousins and Yiwen). Aunt and her husband Yan slept at 930 Long. A few years later as the kids got bigger, Yan built a wobbly attic to meet the urgent need of more space.

All Grandma's possessions were stored in plastic bags stacked up on one side of our full-sized bed. At night she and I cuddled on the other side of the bed. When we had visitors those days, they sat right on our beds. A square dining table, pushed to the wall by the window, had chairs tucked beneath that we pulled out at mealtime.

Grandma took on the task of cooking three meals a day for a family of nine all year round. She would get up before the crack of dawn making breakfast for everyone and then head out to the outdoor market to purchase meat, fish, and vegetables for the day. She always left with an empty bamboo basket. The handle of the basket would leave deep marks on her arm when she came home because it was loaded with stuff. Grandma never went to school to learn how to read and write, but she did the money math in her head so well that nobody could get away with overcharging her. She would spend most of the day processing the raw food, picking out the bad from the good, rinsing, washing, chopping, and cooking. Usually by the time she sat down to eat, there was not much left. Grandma ate a lot of rice to keep her stomach full.

With nine people sardined in a small space, tension flew high. Yan and Grandma didn't get along, and Aunt was sandwiched. Aunt cried a lot those days and threatened to divorce Yan on a few explosive occasions. But they always got back together. In addition to personality conflicts, Yan believed that Grandma favored me and grudged her about it. Every once in a while he would pick at me to start a fight with Grandma. I just wanted to find a hole and hide in it when voices were raised and things started to get ugly.

Grandma would yell at Yan, "You ungrateful son of a gun! I take care of your kids and your family. Is this how you are treating me?"

"I didn't ask you to live with us, your daughter did. And those two girls you brought with you are eating our food and taking our space."

"Have you forgotten that their parents send money every month, and the money is used to buy food for everyone?"

"Money or no money, it doesn't matter … it's getting damn crowded in here!"

"If you don't want us here, we'll move out!"

"Fine!"

"But you're living in my house!" Grandma burst into tears.

"What are you talking about? This is my house!" Yan roared.

On those nights after an emotionally charged argument, Grandma would sit on the bed she and I shared weeping until the wee hours of the night. She would say horrible things, like her life was total misery and she wished it would end soon. The truth was Grandma didn't have a place that she could call home anymore. After a few rounds of shuffling to get everyone else settled, Grandma and Grandpa's humble home was under the name of Yan and Aunt's. Grandpa blamed her for the situation they were in. Grandma had hoped that she and Grandpa would be able to live with Aunt in their old ages. Aunt was her oldest and favorite. The Chinese culture emphasizes children's responsibility to take care of their elderly parents whom they are indebted to for life. The room in 930 Long that Grandma fought to keep belonged to my parents.

They stayed there during their infrequent home visits, and it would also be their retirement home.

I stayed awake and cried silently with Grandma on those long nights, fearful that she would hurt herself in unimaginable ways. I wanted to give her a home that nobody could ever kick her out of. Grandma was my home. Without her, I would be homeless.

In the early morning with puffy eyes, Grandma always got up and continued caring for her family. The last time I saw Grandma, she had been diagnosed with late stage uterine cancer. Taking Jane and Michelle with me, I got on the first available flight to be with her. Her five children decided not to tell her the truth because she had never been seriously sick in her life, and she had always had a fear of dying in the hospital. I didn't know the best way to handle the situation, and I absolutely wouldn't have the heart to tell Grandma she was terminally ill. So I thought I would go along with the plan.

Grandma got out of bed and waited by the door when the elevator took us to the fourth floor.

"Hongwei, you are back! You know I haven't been feeling well." She opened her arms and flung herself at me.

I hugged her tight. She felt so tiny. "Yes. Grandma, I am back, back to see you."

She was thinner than ever. Her skin appeared loosely attached to her bones. She wore light blue cotton pajamas she'd sewn herself. Her hair was still in a bun but hadn't been combed for days.

I spent the most of the next two weeks in this room, chatting with her and reading her Bible stories. Grandma was in pain constantly which she described as menstrual cramps but one hundred times worse. I gave her Tylenol, and, to my surprise, it helped. For the next few days, she was able to get up and sit on the living room sofa for a while. Uncle Mao Mao and I sat with her and we chatted about everyone in the family as well as old neighbors we used to live with. Mao Mao was very sweet to Grandma. He always spoke to her in a soft and kind voice. He brought water, medicine, and meals to her bed, fed her and cleaned up after she ate. They shared a very special mother-son bond. My mother, a former nurse, came almost every day to give Grandma injections and take her blood pressure. She did it professionally but without an element of sweetness. Mother had always resented Grandma, her own mother, for taking her daughter away.

Grandma came to the U.S. after Jane was born and stayed until after Michelle's birth. I took her to church every week, and she accepted Jesus in one of the evangelical gatherings. Those couple of years when she lived with Joe and me were probably the happiest time in her life! How I hoped we could be together like that forever!

My two-week visit flew by too quickly. Most people in my grandma's condition might prefer peace and quiet, but not my grandma. She loved to be surrounded by her grandchildren and great grandchildren. Grandma asked me to let Jane and Michelle stay longer since they were on summer break. I called United Airlines and postponed their return date to two months later. On the day when I had to leave, I took her hands and prayed with her for peace, healing, and eternal life with God. Shortly after lunch, before the taxi van arrived to pick me up, she got up from her bed and followed me around. I didn't want her to see me cry, but it was really hard not to get emotional. When I finally got into the taxi, I lost it and sobbed uncontrollably. As the van started pulling away, I looked back and saw Grandma waving to me from the balcony. My heart was broken to pieces! I knew this would be the last time I was ever going to see her on this earth. It seemed that at last Grandma had found her home when she moved into the new apartment with Uncle Mao Mao six months ago but now she would have to leave again soon. Life could be so cruel sometimes!

Five months later, Grandma passed away. I was in Washington D.C. attending a Christmas Party sponsored by Joe's boss, Mr. Kwan, the owner of a number of small startup companies. The big boss flew all his employees and their families to D.C. for the party. At the time, he probably had no idea that his various businesses were not going to survive another year.

We were trapped at the O'Hare airport Friday evening because of a snowstorm. I just wanted to turn around and go home. It was almost two o'clock in the morning when we eventually landed. In the morning, we took a tour around the city showing Jane and Michelle the White House, the U.S. Capitol building, the Washington Monument, and the Air and Space Museum. The weather was much milder in D.C., which made our little excursion quite pleasant.

For the Christmas party, I wore a tight-fitted red silk qipao with gold embroidery. Jane had on a cute embroidered pink qipao and Michelle wore a light green one. I put up their hair in buns. The three of us looked adorable together. Mr. Kwan must have had spent a fortune on this party. It was a feast with all kinds of delicious food, drinks, desserts, and lots of fun activities for kids. Jane and Michelle had their portraits drawn and face painted. It was good to see the girls having a good time. But for some reason I felt tense and reckless inside. We went back to our hotel room after ten o'clock, and it took me a while to fall asleep. I dreamed of Grandma. She wore a green, flowery apron over her brown sweater she knitted herself. She looked healthy, no sign of pain.

"Hongwei, promise me you will take good care of yourself," she said to me gently.

"I am taking good care of myself, Grandma." I jumped up and down like when I was a little girl.

She took up my hands that for some strange reason looked very coarse.

"Look, you are not taking care of yourself. Promise me you will."

"Yes, I will, I promise."

When I woke up in the morning, I remembered the dream vividly.

We arrived home on Sunday evening. Our voice mailbox was blinking. I pushed the play button "Hongwei, this is Uncle Mao Mao. Grandma may not make it through the day. She wants to talk to you. Call when you get this message." The message was recorded at 9 p.m. on Saturday, Washington D.C. time.

My heart ached.

The light was still blinking. Another message. "Hongwei, Grandma just passed away on December 17th, 1:15 pm. Call when you get this message." This one was recorded at 12:20 a.m. Sunday morning, Washington D.C. time. The year was 2000.

I howled. I was furious at myself for not being there when Grandma wanted to talk to me for the last time. I didn't want to go to D.C in the first place. I felt I needed to be somewhere else the whole time. Now I knew why.

Thankfully my dear Grandma reached out to me in my dream before she had to leave this world. *I love you forever, Grandma! Yes, I promise you I'll take good care of my family and myself.*

Jane peered in and sat down next to me.

"Mommy, you are crying. Do you miss Tai Tai?"

I nodded.

"I miss her very much, too!" She put her head on my shoulder.

Grandma still came to my dreams. Sometimes I spotted her in a crowd, and other times she was much closer. Most of the time she didn't say anything. She just looked at me and smiled.

*

The living condition has improved considerably in Shanghai and all over China since I left the country in 1988. Aunt and Yan purchased an apartment on the outskirts of Shanghai, and my cousin Qiqi's family of three now live in the room once occupied by nine people.

When the taxi took me to the old neighborhood where I grew up, I could hardly recognize it. The first two rows of the Shikumen houses have been demolished, and so now the only thing that separates Qiqi's home from the busy main road is a low concrete wall.

"I think my cousin lives right behind this wall. You may turn here," I directed the taxi driver.

"His house didn't get torn down? That's unfortunate. With this golden location, he could have got paid a boat load of money and buy a nice place somewhere else."

"He'd hoped so too when they announced the highway construction outside his home, but they stopped at his row."

"Oh, well. People like me will never be able to buy a home this lifetime because property value has been going up and up. My income isn't increasing at the same speed. The damn company I work for is taking a bigger bite of my earnings every year. Talk about a shitty life!"

He told me that both he and his wife were from Songjiang, a district of Shanghai, now living in a small rented room in the big city. They worked long, hard hours to support their daughter's college education. Their hope was someday she would get a good job and hopefully make enough money to buy a place for all of them to live in.

Qiqi and his wife, Yang, had their home completely renovated, and the result was amazing. The concrete floor was covered with white tiles. Part of the wall facing the street was knocked down and a door had been put in next to the Shikumen house's main front door. Now they don't have to enter by the back door through the public kitchen. At the back of the room, a neat bathroom with a shower was installed. I remembered how much pain it was sharing the toilet with two other families on the first floor. How smelly the toilet used to be and how often it clogged and overflowed. We used to shower in the public bathhouse once a week in winter and take turns bathing in a round and low wooden bath bucket at home during summertime. Nothing was easy back then, but we didn't know how to live any other way.

They also made a daring effort to increase the height of their residence by digging two feet into the ground. Qiqi remodeled the attic his father built many years ago. It was made of cheap lumber and squeaked every time one of us climbed into it through a shaky ladder. And we had to bend since the attic was less than four feet tall. Now you can stand straight, and there is even a window on the wall facing the street. The structure has been greatly strengthened and improved. Qiqi, Yang, and their daughter sleep in the attic, and the open space downstairs is used for dining and Yang's after-school tutoring business.

"This looks awesome! I can't believe how you guys have transformed this room!" I exclaimed.

"Well, we realized these houses were going to stay. Since we can't afford a new apartment at a good location, we've done the best with what we have." Yang responded modestly, at the same time with a deep sense of pride.

"So how are you guys doing?"

"Oh, the same old, same old," Qiqi flashed a smile.

"How is your mother?"

"Oh, she isn't getting any better. Now she doesn't recognize anyone and has lost the ability to do anything by herself." The smile on Qiqi's face vanished.

Aunt had suffered from Alzheimer's disease for the decade. Last time I saw her, she could no longer talk. Yiwen had warned me beforehand that Aunt might not recognize us. But I saw tears in her eyes the whole time we were there. I wanted to believe that she knew I was there.

"Is your father able to take care of her?"

"They have a part-time helper who bathes her and sometimes cooks for them."

"Qiqi goes there often to help out too," Yang chimed in.

Qiqi is the only one who lives close to his parents. Both his sisters went abroad many years ago, one to South Africa and the other to Singapore. Taking care of a sick person day in and day out for more than ten years must have been tough, and I felt I had to give Yan credit for that.

"I heard you've made some good money in the stock market," I changed the topic to one of Qiqi's favorites.

"Yeah, made some money. The stock market is picking up again and so most people are making money these days, more or less," he chuckled.

At the time China was going through stock market frenzy. Everyone was trading, from the richest to the elderly who lived on a few hundred yuan retirement income. Money seemed easier to come by than ever.

"How is your tutoring business going?" I turned to Yang.

"I have six kids come here regularly. During school year, I try to help them get all their homework done in the three hours they are here. But some days they are given so many assignments that it can get really stressful. Right now it is summer break, so I am reviewing with them what they have learned and teach them next school year material so that they can get ahead."

"How old are these kids?"

"Mostly fifth graders, so about ten years old. You know when they get home, they still have to do their English homework, since I can't help them with that, and prepare for tests and exams for the next day."

"That's a lot of work and pressure for these kids." I thought about my thirteen-year-old Jane and eleven-year-old Michelle who spent on average less than an hour on homework plus half an hour playing piano every day. They sometimes complained about having too much work to do.

Yang agreed. "That's right. Some of them are like little robots, doing things mechanically because they have to."

"What's it like to be a teacher these days?"

"We are asked to teach third grade material from five years ago to first graders. It's like shoving food down their throats whether they like it or not. Our education system is seriously flawed, but we teachers do make good money these days." She admitted she made more money outside the classroom especially from the one-on-one tutoring sessions.

As we talked, little kids in ponytails and colorful t-shirts started to arrive.

"I guess it's time for me to leave." I rose from the chair.

I went out through the back door. The interesting thing was even though every family had significantly improved its own living space, the kitchen still looked gloomy. It felt odd standing in this quiet, familiar kitchen that used to be always so loud and busy. In the old days, it was not only the central place of recipe sharing, socializing, and gossiping for the six families living here, it was also the battleground for inter-family brawls.

The family of three that moved into the room on the second floor directly facing the staircase had no intention to mix with the rest of us from day one. Later it came out in the kitchen gossip that they were nasty and contentious at their old place and so their neighbors cheered to see them move out. The husband and wife were in their early forties with a little boy who seemed to always be sick.

She could be pretty without that permanent frown on her face. He had a round face and nice features, but there was something sinister about him and the stare from behind his glasses sent chills down one's spines. She annoyed the heck out of everyone by constantly clogging one of the two shared sinks. She would turn on the faucet slightly so that the water just trickled in order to prevent her water meter from recording usage. Then she rinsed the vegetable one piece at a time as if she had all the time in the world. Nobody was happy we had to foot her water bill. It didn't take long before fights started to break out. The husband quickly and comfortably slipped into the combative mode, yelling, swearing, charging at his opponent. White foam formed at the corners of his mouth as he got angrier and louder. The whole thing soon escalated to a different level that involved pushing and shoving. At this point, while still going berserk with her verbal attacks in what sounded like a sob, the wife tried to restrain her man from killing someone or being killed.

"Niu Niu, go upstairs and stay in the room!" she shrieked at her skinny son who came downstairs to see what was going on.

Having a common enemy somehow united the other five families by allowing them to overlook the minor frictions amongst themselves.

The intra-family scuffles mostly took place inside the home. But everyone could hear it when voices were raised to a certain level, not just the people who lived in the same unit but also those in the same or adjacent alleys. You could see crowds gathering at the front and back doors of where the explosion was taking place, with people listening, shaking their heads, or whispering to each other.

One hot summer day, I was awoken from my nap to the awful sounds of swearing, furniture breaking and screaming. I jumped out of bed and saw Mr. Yao, whose family lived on the second floor, running down the stairs with his face covered in blood. "He's trying to kill me! My son is trying to kill me," he panted while trying to wipe the blood from his face with his hand. His son's heavy and quick footsteps were not far behind.

Mr. Yao, an outsider in his own home, lived with his wife, two grown sons who were tall and solid, and a daughter. He and his younger son never got along. He was particularly close to his mother. In the rift that just occurred, the younger son punched him on the temple that caused one of the veins to burst. Yan and few other guys stepped in and pulled them apart. Yan then accompanied Mr. Yao to the hospital to get his wound checked.

Putting himself in the authoritative position, Yan scolded the son when they got back from the hospital, "If you have something to say, say it nicely, but don't use your fist. He's your father, for God's sake!" The son gave Yan a dirty look.

\*

The alleys appeared shorter and narrower than how I remembered them. I spent my childhood playing with the other kids in them and emerged as the leader, organizing games, resolving issues among the kids, and assigning roles in different play settings. One year I directed an hour-long performance that included singing, dancing, and a skit and presented it at the home association meeting. Yan was the association chair that year. He didn't criticize the performance I put together which I took as a compliment.

One summer in the mid-seventies, the association obtained a nine-inch black and white TV. The whole neighborhood gathered in the alley in front of the TV every night to watch the only channel that was available back then. People came with their little stool, bamboo fan, and the anticipation to enjoy a good show. The fans weren't only used to provide desperately needed draft in the muggy summer night; they also helped drive away mosquitoes that might otherwise have a gratifying feast.

A mile down the street from Qiqi's home, there's a newly built beautiful garden with lots of trees, colorful plants, walkways, stairways, and strategically placed chairs. It was thoughtfully designed and well maintained in the highly populated residential area. It would have been an awesome playground for my little friends and me even though they didn't put in a play area for kids. We could have played hide and seek, conducted the skipping race, or had our performance rehearsal here. The park seemed like a piece of oasis under the always-gray sky in Shanghai.

The two busiest shopping areas in Shanghai, Nanjing and Huaihai Road, were within walking distance. I had to get on the crossover bridge to go to the other side of the street. From the bridge I saw a sea of black hair down below on Nanjing Road. There were numerous department store buildings, with each floor featuring unique types of products or apparels. The top few levels typically offer entertainment and different style restaurants, along with countless stand-alone restaurants and salons.

Things had changed radically in China, in good and bad ways. With a booming housing and stock market, lots of people had become wealthy in a short period of time. But I sensed recklessness among the sea of people below the bridge. The focus of the nation had shifted to money since the Chinese Economic Reform. The desire to rake in more and faster led some to abandon the basic moral standard. This imposed danger to others. The tension between the rich and poor was also intensifying. The nation had changed too much too quickly, and the psychological impact on those who couldn't adapt as quickly must have been mind-boggling.

*

Jane, Michelle, and I enjoyed a shopping spree at the Taobao City, a fashion and accessory knockoff market. As soon as we walked in, I was dazzled by its size and the vast variety of products. It took up the space of a whole multi-story modern building with escalators and marble floors. The smell of cigarette smoke was annoying, particularly to Jane and Michelle, as it had been in all the public places we'd been.

Chanel handbags instantly caught their eyes.

"How much is this bag?" I pointed to a white bag with the Chanel logo on it.

"Three hundred yuan," the young man replied, studying the three of us.

"One hundred fifty," I counter offered. Yanhua had told me to slash the price by at least fifty percent.

"Come on, ma'am. You've got to let us make some money."

Jane and Michelle looked at the bags longingly.

"Let's go, girls. We'll buy somewhere else." We started walking away.

"Come back. Hey, come back, girls." He ran after us. "Alright, alright, I'll sell it to you for one hundred fifty."

So we went back and bought two bags, a white one for Jane and a black one for Michelle.

Wandering around the maze of shops, we saw all kinds of brand name handbags, suitcases, watches, electronics, toys, shirts, scarves, you name it.

"Come in and take a look," every vendor eagerly invited us in.

Some of them had hidden selling space behind their shops that stores higher end stuff, and they only invite you in if they think you have the money and are serious buyers. A few vendors would take one hundred yuan for the Chanel bags we just bought. I realized we overpaid.

It seems that Chinese aren't the only ones buying knockoff products. Westerners love them too. We spotted many of them in the market. Some of the younger vendors could communicate in broken English, but most of the bargaining was conducted through a calculator.

"How much?" the Westerner would ask.

The vendor would push the buttons on the calculator.

"No, no, too expensive." The Westerner would clear the number and type in a new one.

They would go on and on until a deal was reached. These folks were clearly more sophisticated and persistent bargainers.

One white guy walked away after a few rounds of negotiation with a male merchant. Then an attractive young lady ran after him, held his hands, and led him back to the shop. She didn't speak much English, but it didn't matter since the guy ended up buying the product.

Jane and Michelle had a ball buying all the stuff they had always wanted for a fraction of the regular price. The three of us left the place with a few full shopping bags. But we found out quickly that even though the knockoffs looked like the real thing, they weren't real in terms of quality and durability. You actually get what you pay for. But we thoroughly enjoyed the Chinese-style shopping experience.

Every morning I went to a hair salon across the street from Mao Mao's apartment to get my hair washed and blown out. On the main road within a stretch of a couple of miles, there were at least half a dozen salons, more than a dozen restaurants, a few fruit stands, grocery stores, hardware stores, apparel retailers. If you don't mind the crowdedness and gray sky year-round, the good thing about living in Shanghai is the convenience and variety it offers.

Two pretty young women in white blouses and short, tight red skirts greeted me at the door, "Welcome to Wenfeng Salon!" A dozen or so people working there were busy washing, styling hair, or putting on makeup. It was 8:30 in the morning, and they had just opened the door.

The salon was wide but shallow and had about a dozen stations and three hair-washing sinks. In the back, there were half a dozen private rooms for facial treatments and foot massages.

Mimi came up to me. "Same as yesterday?" She looked young, about sixteen.

"Yes!" I smiled.

I brought my own Matrix shampoo and conditioner. They don't charge extra for the store brand hair products but a crazy amount for the L'Oreal shampoo and conditioner. After washing my hair, Mimi gave me a shoulder, arm, and finger massage, and then cleaned my ears with Q-tips.

I moved to Mr. Zhao's station as usual to get my hair dried and styled. Mr. Zhao was in his late thirties, much older than the rest of the crew. Almost all the employees in this chain salon were from Anhui. The company offered them a dorm room to stay, three meals a day, and a meager salary. They worked long hours, twelve hours a day and six days a week. The young people only went back home to be with their families during the Chinese New Year.

The store manager was talking to the girl behind the reception desk. He waved to another young, tall and slim cosmetician, and she went over and joined the conversation. From the back, I could see him putting his hand on her butt with a squeeze. I motioned for Mr. Zhao to see that.

"These girls think they are in heaven working here. They should think twice about it. We aren't paid enough to do what we do or put up with something like that," he grumbled.

"What's your plan for the future?" I asked.

"What plan can I have? All I know is chopping and styling hair."

"How about open your own shop someday?"

"That would be nice. But I don't know if I'll ever be able to save enough money. My wife is also a hairdresser who works at a different salon. Our daughter is in high school. She's seventeen." Then he muttered hesitantly, "I need to ask you something. A friend of mine wants to hook up my daughter with one of his relatives in America, an older guy. Do you think it's a good idea?"

"No, very bad idea. She should finish high school, go to college, and then decide what she wants to do and who to marry."

"Yeah, you're right. That's why my wife and I are working hard to pay for her education. I hope she can get into college," he sighed.

Mr. Zhao tried again to sell me a hair treatment package, as, according to him, my hair was dry and in bad shape. I politely said no since I had no time to sit in a salon all morning. The morning beauty treatment cost less than $1 with the membership card Yanhua gave me!

*

I hadn't spoken to my mother for three years and certainly wasn't looking forward to being in same time zone with her again. The ill feeling between us began when I was very young.

Grandma took Yiwen and me to visit our parents when I was five years old. I had met them once before when I was one but too young to remember. Aunt liked to query me with a serious look on her face "Who's your mother?" I would point at her with a cute smile on my face, and she would laugh pleasingly. I kind of knew I had another mother who lived somewhere else faraway.

It took seventy-two hours by train to travel from Shanghai to Yun Nan. It was jam packed by people sitting on the hard seats or standing, goods in big sacks, and small animals in cages. It smelled like wet armpits. Every time the train stopped, small vendors swarmed to the windows offerings boxed meals, snacks, and fruits. As we went further south, the soil turned from yellow to red and the people appeared at the windows appeared more filthy and desperate.

There was no space to walk to the toilet when I had to pee. Grandma had to lift me up to pee outside the window. When it got too dusty and windy to open the widow, she would raise me over her head and pass me to the person in the next row. This continued on until I was close enough to the toilet to squeeze in, and then I would be transported all the way back.

When we finally got off the train after three days and nights, my sister and I looked like we'd just climbed out of the garbage dumpster. Our faces and hair were covered with dirt, and we stank. Grandma told us to stay put and wait for our parents. Then we saw a man and a woman walking towards us with big smiles on their faces. The woman bore a resemblance to Grandma but was slightly taller. She wore a wrinkled, loosely fit light blue top and blue pants, her short black hair clipped behind her ears. The man had dark and thick eyebrows and wore a gray Mao suit. He was unhealthily thin, walking with his hands behind his back. As the woman fastened her steps, he trailed behind and eventually stopped and looked on, grinning.

The excessively enthusiastic woman bent down and handed my sister and me each an apple.

"Thank you, Auntie." I took the apple and smiled at her.

"No, that's your mother," Grandma nudged me. "Call her Mommy."

I hid behind Grandma's legs, embarrassed. The smile on my mother's face disappeared, only to be replaced by an unspoken sadness and disappointment. Mother took Yiwen's hand and walked ahead of us. Grandma and I followed. I had pissed off my mother!

My parent's two-bedroom apartment looked spacey but temporary. There wasn't much furniture, other than a few beds, just an enormous wardrobe in their bedroom, a sofa, and a dining set. None of the furniture was painted, although my father boasted of the high quality of the wood. They never planned to stay in Yun Nan for very long but ended up living here for almost twenty-five years!

The two months with my parents were utterly miserable for me. Mother didn't allow me to leave the table until I finished everything she put in my bowl. In Shanghai, there were so such ridiculous rules. Grandma still fed me at the age of four. I would be jumping and skipping faraway from the house with Grandma in tow, a bowl and spoon in her hands. Mother wanted to set the boundary, but I didn't want to have anything to do with this strange, crazy woman. I got even more clingy to Grandma and absolutely refused to call the other woman Mommy. She got more and more agitated as each day went by. One day it erupted like a volcano. She grabbed me, pulled down my pants, and continuously whacked my butt like a mad woman. Father sat on his bamboo couch with a grave look on his face, Grandma stood by crying. My father always sat on that bamboo couch resting. He suffered from severe eczema, and his heavy drinking and smoking didn't help. Mother took care of him like a baby and did everything around the house. "I am your mother. You have to listen to *me*!" Mother screamed hysterically.

"No, you're not my mother! I will *not* listen to you!" I shrieked back.

After the explosive incident, I tried to stay as far away from my mother as I possibly could. If we were in the same room, I simply didn't acknowledge her presence or have any eye contact with her. On numerous occasions, she accused Grandma of spoiling me and not raising me the way she would have liked.

"If you don't like the way I am raising her, why don't you do it yourself?" Grandma eventually lashed out after enduring days of her daughter's criticism.

The tension became too much for a five-year-old. I was afraid Grandma would leave me behind to live with my mother, which would be a living hell. Mother's face closed every time she looked at me, and there was growing frustration and irritation in her voice when she addressed me. I wanted to go back to Shanghai so badly. It was not the best place in the world, but much better than this.

Much to my relief, my parents decided to keep only Yiwen with them. She would attend elementary school in Yun Nan. They sent her back to Shanghai a year later because my parents realized she could get a much better education in Shanghai. The day finally arrived for Grandma and me to leave. I was over the moon! The pain and despair on my mother's face revealed that she knew she had lost me, maybe forever.

For the next three days, everyone on the train told Grandma that I was the sweetest and best behaving little girl they had ever seen.

When Michelle reached school age, my father had long passed away. I asked mother if she would like to come to America. To my surprise she agreed without giving it any thought. Just like Mother asked Grandma to take care of my sister and me, I thought it would be good for Jane and Michelle to come home to their Grandma after school, and it would also be nice to have someone other than me cook for the family. Cooking just wasn't my thing. When my mother first arrived, everything was fine. We were polite to each other and exchanged a few words every day. Jane and Michelle liked her, which was important to me. But her presence had an oppressive effect on me and gradually made me feel physically sick. Mother's facial expression and tone of voice opened the floodgate of painful memories that had been buried deep in my memories. Soon I shut down and fell back to the default mode of dealing with my mother. I'd ignore her with no eye contact. The silence drove her nuts. Many times I caught a glimpse of her standing by the kitchen window staring blankly.

She told some older women from church that she was only here to pay a debt.

On a Saturday before Easter Sunday, Jane and Michelle were at friends' houses. I awoke from my nap by weeping coming from my mother's room. Joe and I rushed in.

"What's the matter, mom?" Joe asked.

"I'm just sad, heartbreaking," she sobbed, grabbing her chest.

Then she turned to me. "Hongwei, I know I haven't been a good mother to you. I'm here trying to make it up to you."

*Is my mother actually apologizing?*

"Well, I'm—I'm ..." This came as a total surprise, and I was lost for words.

She continued before anything meaningful came out of my mouth. "I can't change what happened in the past. But I am your mother, and I gave birth to you. Can you just treat me like one?"

*If you are my mother, why haven't you acted like one?*

"Well, I'm trying. It's not ..." I mumbled.

"Great! Action speaks louder than words. I'm going to expect some changed behavior from you. Okay?"

She wiped away her tears.

*How come this woman never understands that she can't demand me to love and accept her as my mother?*

I looked at her and walked out of the room. I couldn't give my mother what she wanted. But seeing how miserable she was, I knew I had to release her from paying back the debt. I had no right to make her life a living hell in my home.

Mother left on Mother's Day. No reconciliation took place between us. As a matter of fact, I was even more turned off by her whole act. She used to beat me in order to force me to call her Mommy, now she begged. Neither worked.

Yiwen informed me of a new apartment construction across the street from her home. Joe and I decided to secure a unit for my mother. So she went back to Shanghai with something to look forward to: a new home very close to Yiwen and spending more time with her granddaughter Lee. By the time the construction finished and before mother even moved in, the value of the property already doubled. What was really nice about my mother's new apartment was that she could see my sister's apartment from her balcony. So she knew they were home from work when the lights were turned on.

I hadn't picked up the phone to call my mother since the day she left Chicago. If Grandma were still alive, I would have taken Jane and Michelle to Shanghai every year. So at the ages of twelve and ten, this was only their third trip to China. Yiwen invited us to stay at her place for a few days so that her daughter Lee and my kids could get acquainted. Lee is a couple years older than Jane. Even though my sister never did well in school, Lee was an overachiever, and her parents were very proud of that. Lee called her parents by their first and last names, and they answered to her willingly and happily. The three of them resided in a three-bedroom apartment in Pudong, the east bank of the Huangpu River, across from the city center of Shanghai. Pudong has grown rapidly since the 1990s and emerged as China's financial and commercial hub.

I don't see the close resemblance everyone else sees in Yiwen and me. For one thing, she is half a head shorter than I and is loud and unpolished. Personality-wise, we have nothing in common either. Yiwen and I both had a rough childhood living with Grandma under the roof of Aunt and Yan. Yiwen probably had it worse because she was not on Grandma's good book. We developed entirely different survival mechanisms. Each time Yiwen got into trouble and was punished for it, she would wail and throw a tantrum like it was the end of the world. But her intense emotion disappeared as fast as it came. After the storm passed, she would act like nothing had happened. It was like watching a tornado swirl by without leaving any debris behind. For some reason, Yiwen was closer to my cousins, Jie Jie and Duan Duan, than she was to me. Oftentimes they would gang up on me. Once she tore up all the stamps I had collected. I was fuming and we both got into trouble for that one. She never acted like a big sister.

My sister flunked the national entrance exam for college and stayed at home a full year to supposedly do nothing but study. She did worse the second time. Our mother got fed up and wanted her to find a job and support herself. She was offered a job as a worker in a textile factory. It was a dusty and noisy environment, and she had to work a different shift every week, which totally threw off her sleeping pattern. In her late twenties, she finally got wiser and started taking accounting classes at night. Now she worked as the head accountant in a Mazda dealership.

I was not able to let things go as easily as Yiwen. Whenever I got hurt, I would hold onto it, chew on it, and somehow turn it to a motivational force. When I reached school age, I overheard Yan saying to Grandma, "Maybe you should hold Hongwei back a year. She isn't ready for school yet. She won't survive a day without you holding her hand."

I resented him for saying that. Crying silently, I vowed I would do better in school than any of his children. I studied in that crowded small room when everyone else in the family was watching TV, chatting, and laughing. After a while I couldn't concentrate without the distinctive background noises. When I had to take a test, I would wake up very early in the morning, standing under a flicking fluorescent light tube that had turned black on both ends, making sure I understood the material I was to be tested on. I flourished academically, got into one of the best high schools in Shanghai and was the only one out of the five kids who made it to college.

Mother was all smiles when she entered Yiwen's apartment. "I went to the market and got you guys breakfast. They are still hot. Come and eat! Come, come, come," she announced enthusiastically. Mother stood by the girls and watched gratifyingly as we ate the breakfast she brought us.

"Eat, eat, eat more." She kept on pushing more food onto Jane and Michelle's plates.

Part of me wanted to say something nice to her like, "Thank you for getting us breakfast!" or even "Thank you, Mom, for getting us breakfast!" After all she was seventy-three years old. Time was running out for me to give her what she had wanted from me all her life. But I couldn't and wouldn't. All I could remember was her explosive anger and her repeated beatings. My parents retired and moved back permanently when I was in college. Mother couldn't smack me around anymore, and so her tactics changed from physical to verbal abuse. She called me a whore one time and angrily prophesized that I was going to die before the age of fifty after finding me passed out in the bathroom of 930 Long.

After many years of struggle and praying, I had arrived at a place where I no longer hated her for ruining my childhood. I was willing to forgive her as Jesus had forgiven me. But I couldn't forget what she had done, which meant I wouldn't allow her to come into my life and hurt me again. Distance is the key to my relationship with my mother.

*

The height of our trip was the family reunion Joe and I planned and hosted in a fancy restaurant on Nanjing Road. Seventy family members and relatives from both sides were expected to show up. He and I had been looking forward to the event long before our arrival in Shanghai because we had a special message to share.

Adding to the excitement were two special guests: Gjyn and Mitch from Australia. They used to be my English teachers in college. Gjyn and Mitch first came to Shanghai East China University of Science and Technology in 1986 with their cute three-year-old, blue-eyed, blond-haired little girl Esther. At the time, not too many Westerners lived in Shanghai, and so they, especially Esther, became the attraction wherever they went.

Gjyn literally lit the room when she turned up for the first class. "Oh, my, what a warm day!" She put her things down on the teacher's desk and started taking off her red sweater. "How are you doing class?" She stared at us with squinted eyes and an exaggerated happy face shaped smile. None of our Chinese teachers acted like that. We laughed. Gjyn was indeed very different. Her class was much more interactive and she was very personal. She was the first adult I had ever met who wasn't afraid of letting her wide range of facial expressions reveal her internal thoughts and feelings. Gjyn also told you things as they were. Gjyn came into my world like a fresh breath of air when I lived behind a thick mask as everyone else. But there was something else about her that really caught my attention.

So after a few more classes, I approached her. "Gjyn, what makes you so happy all the time?"

"I'm happy all the time, really?"

"Yeah! You laugh all the time. You're full of energy and passion, and you really care about your students."

"I have Jesus. Jesus loves me, and he loves you, too." She looked into my eyes and smiled a beautiful smile.

"Who is Jesus?"

"Come to our apartment this evening, and I'll tell you who he is."

"I'll be there!" I was anxious to see what a foreigner's home would look like.

Their furnished two-bedroom apartment was on the second floor of the professor's residence building on the far end of the campus. It looked cozy and spacious. There were a few pictures of Esther on the end tables in the living room. Other than the colorfulness and simplicity, I looked no different than any other apartments in the building. But something was distinctively missing: the lasting smell of Chinese cooking!

Gjyn and Mitch welcomed me to their home with a radiant smile. I sat on the grey fabric sofa with Gjyn and Mitch took the love seat. Gjyn handed me a Bible that had been on the coffee table. "This is the Bible, God's word. Jesus is the Son of God who came to the world to save us. He died on the cross for you and for me so that we can be reconciled with God. Hongwei, God loves you and you are very special in his eyes!" Gjyn's long eyelashes were sparkling with tears. "He wants you to be his child, Hongwei! Someday all those who believe in him will live in Heaven with God forever!"

*Wow! I am special in God's eyes, really? God sent Gjyn and Mitch all the way from Australia to tell me he loves me? If God the creator of the universe loves me and wants me to be with him forever, there could only be one possible response to his invitation.*

"Yes, I want to be a child of God," I declared.

Gjyn beamed and in tears held my hands and led me in a prayer to accept Jesus Christ as my personal savior.

The next morning I woke up early and ran ten laps in the track field. Everything seemed different: the trees were greener, the air fresher, and the new life in me was budding!

I began having regular Bible study with Gjyn and Mitch. Soon Joe and a couple of my classmates joined. Every once in a while, we would be interrupted by knocks on the door. We would have to hide our Bible behind the sofa cushions since it was illegal to have unregistered religious gatherings.

It took Joe much longer to convert. He asked many questions such as, "What does it mean that we are sinners? My father was the best person I've ever known in the world, and he was definitely not a sinner." "How could a virgin give birth to a baby?" "Is there any scientific proof that God and Jesus really exist?" His biggest hurdle was how a loving and powerful God could allow his father to die from a vicious disease namely lung cancer at the age of sixty-three.

Joe and I built a lasting relationship with the O'Tooles. I invited them to have lunch with my family at Aunt's home. Grandma spent a week straightening the place. I had never seen it so neat before, and I didn't know it could possibly get this clean. Gjyn and Mitch ate almost all the food put in their plates with a smile. Now I knew that some of dishes might be too authentic for Westerners. At the time we only wanted to present to them our best. They also spent a weekend at Joe's mother's house in Pudong. It was a five-bedroom brick house with an old-fashioned kitchen and family room. Joe's parents had the house built for their five male offspring, one room for each. None of the boys ended up living there due to its distant location from the center of Shanghai. It was built in the early sixties with no sewer system and thus no flushing toilet. In its place was a wooden pail with a lid. It was not a problem for me since I was used to the overflowing smelly toilet. Upon arrival, Joe took them on a tour around the house. As soon as we got into the room with the wooden pail, Joe and I looked at each other and realized it could be a problem for the O'Tooles especially for Esther. There was a moment of awkwardness, but they managed gracefully. Esther loved the little puppy my mother-in-law was raising at the time. Gjyn even offered to pay for the puppy's expenses so that Esther could come back and visit it from time to time.

Gjyn, Mitch, and Esther came to see us when lived in Long Island, New York and celebrated Jane's first birthday with us. Eleven years had passed since that last visit!

I looked around anxiously the minute we stepped into the restaurant building. No, they were not in the lobby. The escalator took us to the ninth floor where our family reunion reservation had been made. There they were, sitting at the waiting area! Gjyn's blond hair had turned silvery. Mitch was thinning out on the top, and his big mustache looked gray which matched his hair.

"Hongwei!" Gjyn spotted me too. I ran into her embrace.

"It's so good to see you again!" I exclaimed.

"It's wonderful to see you too, Hongwei! It's been a long time." Gjyn was ecstatic.

Mitch rubbed his hands together, beaming.

Guests started to trickle in. Joe and I stood by the door to greet everyone. Close family from my side included my Big Uncle, Uncle Mao Mao, Uncle DD, cousin Qiqi, Yiwen, and my mother; from Joe's side: his three brothers, two sisters, and his mom. My two other cousins weren't around at the time. Yan and Aunt couldn't make it due to Aunt's condition.

Big Uncle, who was dressed as a girl by Grandma, was now a well-known lawyer in Shanghai. But clearly his wife still ruled. Her voice reached my ears before she and uncle were in sight. "I can tell whether a restaurant is good or not just by sniffling. If there's a strong aroma of artificial ingredients, it just can't be good." She spoke with an authoritative tone. Then she addressed my uncle. "Remember not to eat any beef because they inject the cows with all kinds of bad stuff. Okay?"

You couldn't tell Big Uncle was a big shot by looking at him. His wife hadn't updated his wardrobe for at least ten years. The crease on uncle's collar was tearing and the collar had lost its stiffness. There was also a visible patch on his sleeve. Their twenty-year-old daughter, Catherine, in contrast, was in style.

Uncle Mao Mao and Yanhua came with their grown son who still lived at home. They had both retired. Their son spent all his free time hiding his room playing computer games. Neither Yanhua nor Mao Mao was in good health. Mao Mao had long suffered from gastroptosis and appeared gaunt, and Yanhua was a breast cancer survivor who'd also had multiple open-heart surgeries. Yanhua and I shared a more intimate relationship than I did with most of my own family members, as she is not only my uncle's wife but also Joe's older sister.

Uncle DD married late since he spent most of his youth working in Jilin, a province located in northeastern part of China, as a result of the Down to the Countryside Movement, in which urban youths were transferred to rural regions to be reeducated. Now he was a government functionary working at a subdistrict office of Shanghai, a job envied and eyed by many. His wife was a homemaker spending most of the day playing Mahjong with her friends for money.

My mother arrived with Yiwen's family. She wore her gray hair in a Chinese bob. Her teeth were noticeably stained, and her facial expression softened somewhat. She glanced at me cautiously, but her smile brightened up at the sight of Jane and Michelle.

"Wow! You've grown so much. Beautiful young ladies, and you've got some meat on your bones now. That's good, that's good."

Almost everyone commented that Jane and Michelle had gained weight.

"Why does everyone think we are fat?" Michelle complained.

"It's actually a compliment. In the old days, food was scarce. So if someone said you were getting fat, it implied that your family was in good shape," I explained.

She didn't quite believe me. "In fact, Chinese people greet each other by 'Have you eaten?' instead of 'How are you?'" I continued.

"Whatever." Michelle rolled her eyes.

Joe's oldest brother showed up with his 10-month-old grandson on his shoulder, followed by his wife, son, and daughter-law, all smiling.

Rende, his third oldest brother, had become an entrepreneur. Like my Uncle DD, he was assigned to Heilongjiang at the age of sixteen to receive his reeducation working as a lumberman. He met someone there who was also from Shanghai, and they got married and had a daughter. After the whole family transferred back to Shanghai, Rende became the co-owner of a textile trading company with a couple of friends from Heilongjiang. Business was picking up, and he was very busy traveling around the country soliciting orders. It seemed that Rende had lost quite a bit of weight. He contributed it to quitting smoking.

Xuehua, Joe's third oldest sister, was even louder than Yiwen. Her laugher vibrated the hallway. Xuehua and her husband used to live on a meager budget. Now their situation had improved drastically because they had became owners of multiple apartments. Her mother-in-law's old house in the suburban Shanghai had been demolished to make room for new apartment buildings. She was compensated with a number of apartment units, which she divided between her two sons. Xuehua rented her units out for additional income plus the property value had been following a steep upward trend, which made a lot of people very rich. Xuehua had always been a happy and content person. Now she had even more reasons to be happy.

My mother-in-law was eighty-five years old but still in perfect health. She had never been on any kind of diet or taken any medication. Her daily routine included exercise, reading, all afternoon mahjong playing, and TV watching after dinner. Losing both her husband and oldest daughter to lung cancer didn't seem to alter her positive outlook towards life. Maybe that, along with an active life style, contributed to her long and healthy life.

Everyone arrived and quickly filled the six reserved tables. Our corner of the restaurant was bustling with greetings and small talk. Our families were clearly growing older, lots of gray hair and bald heads. Close to a dozen young folks and Bide's grandson added some youthfulness to the mix.

The one-child policy introduced in 1978 along with the rapid economic growth since the late 80s had produced a different breed – The Chinese style X-Generation.

Fuerdai, Rich 2G, referred to those born in the 80s and with an inheritance of millions (US dollars) from their parents who had been the first-generation entrepreneurs as a result of the economic reform. According to a report released by Merrill Lynch in 2004, there were close to a-quarter-million multi-millionaires in Mainland China and far more millionaires, which made the Rich 2G quite a sizable population.

It was estimated that 20% of the Rich 2G were outstanding due to the rich resources provided by their parents and their own willingness to work hard and smart. Some had even expanded their parents' family business into high-tech areas such as software development and advertisement media. 50% had turned prodigal, their lives characterized by boredom, depression, and spending without restraint. The rest were just mediocre.

On the other end of the spectrum are the Poor 2G. They were the second generation of the workers or farmers who hadn't been able to take advantage of the economic reform and remained poor. The starting point of Poor 2G was much lower than their peers. Lack of education wasn't the only problem this group faced. Even if they did manage to get into and graduate from college, the opportunities presented to them could still be very limited. Poor 2G greatly resented the unfair competition and those who were entitled to the abundance and privileges of life.

Typically parents of Poor 2G were willing do whatever it took to make their children's lives better than their own. As a result, Poor 2G were losing the determination and hardworking spirit their parents possessed. Uncle Mao Mao had told me a story about a peasant couple who managed to send their only child to a fine boarding junior high school by saving every penny they made. Instead of studying hard, their son frequently climbed over the wall of the campus at night to have fun. One late night, he was about to do the same thing, but he saw something that caused him to turn around abruptly. The kid changed from that night on and started to devote most of his free time to schoolwork. Instead of failing, he excelled but kept mum about what had happened that night. At graduation, he finally told his classmates the truth that they had been dying to know. That night at the top of the wall, this young man saw down below his dad huddling up and dozing off. His dad had received his letter to send more money. Instead of spending a little to stay in a motel, his father chose to sleep on the street so that his son could have more money. The son was awakened right at that moment and realized what he had to do to deserve the sacrifice his parents were making for him.

The Bureaucratic 2G referred to those whose parents were in power. These days anyone who worked for the government held the envious position. They got lots of perks on top of a very comfortable salary and benefits. The deals conducted under the table easily made their salary insignificant.

Giving and taking bribery had become a widely accepted way of conducting business in China and a daunting social problem.

The majority of the X-generation was neither very rich nor very poor. Surprisingly there was no official name for this large group. So I'd call them Ordinary 2G although they preferred to be categorized as Poor 2G because compared to the Rich 2G, they felt terribly underprivileged and deprived.

The dozen Ordinary 2G in our families had been doing averagely well, and this was what average looked like. Most of them were working and long hours (a common workplace requirement in Shanghai), not married (some not even dating in their 30s) and living at home, and their parents still took care of them as if they were teens. They spent a lot of the spare time sitting in front of the computer playing games or making cyber connections. They did have big dreams but no step-by-step plan to achieve them. Living at home was very comfortable, and it made the Ordinary 2G lazy and unmotivated. They complained that opportunities weren't as readily available as ten years ago. They knew that they wouldn't be able to afford a place of their own without their parents' generous and sacrificial help.

Looking around at the young people sitting at the tables, I couldn't help but wondering if they were still unwilling and unprepared to leave their nest in their late 20s, when they would ever grow up to serve others and become the driving force of the society.

Jane and Michelle settled at the table with Gjyn and Mitch, and I could see that Gjyn was making a connection with them the same way she did with me many years ago.

Shortly after the appetizers were served, Joe and I stood up and welcomed everyone. Since Jane, Michelle, and I had not been back to Shanghai for five years and because we had not seen some of the relatives for over fifteen years, Joe and I thought it would be a good icebreaker to show some pictures of how our family had transformed over the years. The waiters and waitresses all turned their eyes to the screen while serving.

Then the time came for delivering the special message, the reason why we got everyone together. Taking a deep breath, I told the story of my tubal pregnancy and how God had saved my life by stopping me from getting on the plane. How happy I was to see everyone again and how Joe and I had prayed for the salvation of our entire clan. Mitch reinforced my testimony with a short sermon about the true meaning of life and God's plan for our salvation. I stood next to him and translated his message.

By now the twelve main dishes had been served and the waiters and waitresses all lined up against the wall, listening attentively. I saw curiosity, amazement, and question marks on people's faces. There was an urge in me to ask for a show of hands if anyone wanted to accept Jesus as His personal savior that day, but that would be illegal. After all, this was a family reunion, not a registered religious gathering. So the lunch gathering ended the Chinese style: people boxed leftovers, said goodbye, and parted ways.

We gave our close family members copies of the Bible when we visited them individually. The seeds had been planted, and we were longing for a big harvest someday.

*

The baby question did come to mind from time to time. Joe and I couldn't decide. I simply couldn't deliberately plan to go through it again, knowing all the risks and pain it could invoke. So we left it to God.

The first three pregnancies just happened. It didn't take any planning on our part. I told Joe and myself that if I were to have a baby again, it would have to happen the same way. Meanwhile, there were always babies to hug and hold at church. After the Sunday worship when we gathered for lunch in the junior high school's gym, I would usually walk around with someone's baby in my arms.

After returning to Chicago from Shanghai in the middle of July, I plunged into the final preparation for Living Water's annual summer retreat only three weeks away. Promotional pitch to the congregation was made back in May. Meetings had been held, tasks assigned to individuals, and different Bible study groups and the registration process were well underway. I had also set up various checkpoints to make sure everyone was moving forward as planned. Since this was my third time coordinating the event, it had been smooth sailing until that Thursday morning when the retreat was scheduled to go live in the afternoon.

I was working from home that morning and planned to leave for the retreat site with the invited speaker, Pastor Wang, after lunch. A young couple volunteered to pick him up from the O'Hare airport. My cell phone started ringing early. The couple couldn't locate Pastor Wang! They had been circling around the arrival terminals a few times hoping to spot him. By now they had parked their car and went inside. Still no sign of the speaker. They wanted to know what to do. After a chain of phone calls, I finally got Pastor Wang's cell phone number, but he wasn't answering.

I was about to panic: without the speaker, there would be no retreat! But there was another reason to rattle me even more: my period was late again! I had been trying to put it on the backburner for a couple of days, and now I just had to find out. So I headed for Jewel-Osco and grabbed the first pregnancy test I saw.

On the way home, another coworker called to inform me she had a family emergency, and I would therefore have to find someone else to take her place for checking people in. *Okay, I'll deal with this later, but first I'll have to find out if I am pregnant again.*

As soon as my car entered the garage, I turned off the engine and rushed to the bathroom where I quickly ran the test without reading the instructions. My cell phone was ringing again in my purse. I ran back to the study and picked it up. It was Pastor Wang! He had got my message and was calling me back. I gave him the number of the couple who were looking for him. One issue resolved, phew!

Returning to the bathroom, I looked at the pregnancy test lying on the tile floor: no lines! *What the heck does that mean?* I read the instruction and found out it meant the test was invalid. *Somebody must be playing a joke on me, and it's not funny!* Out of the blue, I started to giggle. *God definitely has a sense of humor. He is trying to tell me to slow down and calm down.* I got the message and took a deep breath.

I went back to Jewel and this time picked out a twin pack just in case something got messed up again. Back in my bathroom, I did everything in slow motion, laid the test on the cadmium green tile vanity top and waited. *I can't be pregnant. Joe and I have been careful. Maybe the lateness is due to traveling, time zone change and the pressure to get things ready for summer retreat. After all I am thirty-eight years old with only one good tube. The chance of getting pregnant is close to zero.*

I had a chat with my high school classmate, Cathy, just a couple of days ago. She had been trying to get pregnant for her first baby. Cathy asked me if I had made a decision about another baby.

"I think I'm done. This is it," I told her.

"Are you sure?" She wanted me to have another one.

Cathy got pregnant shortly after my last failed pregnancy, but unfortunately it turned out to be abnormal as well and was terminated by her doctor immediately. She was told that based on the blood test results, it was very likely to be tubal. She had been trying to get pregnant again ever since.

I peeked at the test then looked away, my faced blushed deep red, and my heart pounded faster against my chest. I repeated the test, and the result was the same. Pacing with my knees knocking together, I tried to figure out what all this meant.

The pain I had to endure when my tube ruptured had become dull after nearly two years. But now I was living it again, real time. I had to gasp for air.

*What if something goes wrong again? What if this turns out to be a molar pregnancy? What if the baby isn't healthy?*

My phone rang. The couple had picked up Pastor Wang, and they were on their way to lunch.

*But who gets pregnant at the age of thirty-eight with only one good tube without even trying? This has to be gift, a gift from God!*

In my heart I knew I was going to have this baby. If this was a gift from above, the only right thing to do was take it with thankfulness.

I had to tell Joe. He had back-to-back meetings all morning. I anxiously waited for him to call me back.

Finally my home phone rang. I picked it up before the first ring stopped.

"Wow, you picked up that phone really fast. What's up?" Joe chuckled.

"Guess what?"

"What?"

"I am pregnant!"

Without the slightest hint of hesitation, Joe exclaimed, "Congratulations, baby! I am so happy, so happy for us!"

Hearing his joyful voice did the magic for me. *Yes, I can and will go through it again!*

I wanted Dr. Simon to be my obstetrician this time. He had separated from Dr. Chang's group and opened his independent practice. I called his office. Since he now belonged to a different healthcare group, I would have to switch my family doctor and the girls' pediatrician if I chose him. The impact seemed too great.

Dr. Chang was somewhat inexperienced. Some of my friends encouraged me to sue her for negligence. If there was any suspicion that my pregnancy could be tubal, she should have put a rush on the second blood test result instead of waiting another twenty-four hours for it to come back. Then it would have been a different surgery, and I would not have had to lose all that blood or possibly my life. I contemplated it and decided not to pursue a lawsuit. I was just happy to be alive and more interested in moving forward than looking backward. About a year ago, a woman I barely knew approached me in church and told me that Dr. Chang suspected her of having a tubal pregnancy and sent her to the hospital for blood work. She specifically instructed her not to leave the hospital without the report of the blood test. This woman's tubal rupture was avoided. It seemed that Dr. Chang could learn from past experiences in her medical practices. So I decided to stick with her.

I called her office and left a message "Hi, Dr. Chang. This is Linda Xu. Hope you still remember me. I think I am pregnant again. I'll be away this weekend. Will call you back on Monday."

I went to pick up the speaker from the restaurant, and together we headed toward the retreat site. I was over the moon! After some small talk, I quickly opened up to Pastor Wang whom I had never met before about my last pregnancy, how I desired to serve God more after that, and the brand new baby in my womb. Somehow I turned into a chatterbox, and Pastor Wang listened graciously, smiling, and nodding from time to time. "Your experience is quite amazing. I want to pray for you." He prayed that God would bless Joe and me with a healthy baby and that he would continue to use me as his vessel to further his kingdom.

Our retreat was held in one of the dorm buildings of Northern Illinois University. The big dinning room in the lobby was divided into two equal sections, half for serving meals and half as the meeting place for the Mandarin congregation. The children's program was offered in the classrooms and sitting areas of the lobby. In the basement, there was a fitness room, a pool, and a conference room where the English congregation gathered. Everything was pretty much in one place, which was really convenient. Only some of the afternoon recreational activities such as basketball, volleyball, and bowling were held in other buildings. We called our annual summer retreat a spiritual feast since in those four days we were separated from the rest of the world and its worries, focusing only on God's word and fellowship with one another.

Joe arrived late Friday afternoon. He could tell by the way I was running around that I was tired but in high spirits. I usually couldn't sleep well during the retreat because the evening sharing and prayer session after the speaker's message typically ended late at night and the dorm could get quite noisy with people coming and going. Sometimes we could also hear the train whistling in the middle of the night. I had always been a light sleeper—anything woke me up. As the event coordinator, I had to keep an eye on everything and handle emergency situations whenever they arose. Just hours ago before lunch, a dad went to pick up his five-year-old daughter from the children's program but found her missing from the classroom. He went ballistic and yelled at the American family that was taking care of our pre-school kids. Fortunately, the girl was quickly found. She was in the building but wandered away.

For the next couple of days, Joe was keeping an eye on me. If I left something behind and went back to trace it, I would see him in a distance with my stuff in his hands. When I finally made my way to the dinning room, he would have saved a seat for me and had my food ready in a tray next to where he sat. *What a guy! What would I do without him?* The thought of raising another baby with him made me feel warm and fuzzy inside.

The summer retreat ended with a big bang. I was inspired to hear testimony after testimony about how people's lives had transformed in the last few days. Everyone was looking forward to applying what they'd learned to real life situations. Many people complimented my team and me for doing an incredible job. Mission accomplished! Now I could go home, have a good night sleep, and make an appointment to see Dr. Chang.

*

It turned out Dr. Chang did remember me because my answer machine recorded five calls from her office. Dr. Chang herself left the last one. "Linda, I need to see you ASAP. Please call on Monday to schedule an appointment."

I called from work on Monday and made an appointment for Tuesday. Dr. Chang prescribed blood test and ultrasound. The blood test indicated high hormone level, which suggested a normal pregnancy. I shared the baby news with Cathy.

"That's great! I hope I'll get pregnant right after you, just like last time," she said hopefully.

My disdain for ultrasounds had grown over the years. I only drank half of the required amount of water hoping I'd be able to hold it until the end of the exam. This time, at the Hinsdale hospital, the technician looked like she'd just graduated from college. I was only five weeks pregnant which didn't make it easy for her to locate the embryo.

"Oh, not again!" I moaned.

The young technician solicited help from a couple of her colleagues. Joe stood by my side holding my hand as they talked amongst themselves trying to find a needle in a haystack.

"I think that's it—move to the right just a little. Yes, that's it!" the male technician exclaimed. "You can even see the heartbeat!"

I turned my head. There was a tiny spot on the screen that expanded and contracted, expanded and contracted. *Yes! The baby is in the right place this time! This is a beautiful start!* A hearty smile spread across Joe's face.

The technicians told us that the embryo at this stage was the size of an apple seed that could be difficult to detect and thus seeing the heartbeat was definitely a bonus. We left the hospital hardly able to contain our excitement. We were really going to have a baby!

Cathy did become pregnant four weeks after I conceived.

\*

During a routine checkup at week thirteen, Dr. Chang had some troubling news for me. She looked hesitant and uncertain, "Linda, the blood test shows that you have antibody in your system which can be harmful to the baby."

"What is antibody?" *The blood test was done at least a month ago. Why is she bringing this up now?*

"It means you have Rh-negative blood. If the baby is Rh-positive, it can cause hemolytic disease of the newborn."

"Wait, I don't understand any of this. Where did I get the antibodies?"

"I am not sure about that either." She looked puzzled.

"Could it be from the blood transfusion?"

"Yeah, that has to be it!" A light bulb lit up in her head.

"Please explain to me in layman's terms what this means."

"Okay. During pregnancy, red blood cells from the unborn baby can cross into the mother's bloodstream through the placenta. If the mother is Rh-negative, her immune system treats the Rh-positive fetal cells as if they were a foreign substance and makes antibodies against the fetal blood cells. These anti-Rh antibodies may cross back through the placenta into the developing baby and destroy the baby's circulating red blood cells."

"So exactly what happens to the baby?"

"The baby may suffer from severe jaundice or blood contamination."

"Is there anything we can do to prevent that from happening?"

"Well, if the baby is also Rh-negative, the problem goes away. We need do a blood test on your husband."

Joe tested Rh-positive, meaning our baby had a fifty percent chance of being positive. Dr. Chang said I would have to take regular blood tests to monitor the antibody level.

"This is also the time to perform the amniocentesis test for detecting chromosome abnormalities."

I knew this test involved the needle that could potentially harm the fetus. I jumped in before she finished her explanation. "I don't want to take it. It won't matter either way."

She looked at me for a second and then replied, "Okay."

Joe and I were concerned about the antibody risk. We researched online and read blogs posted by people who had experience with it. The good news was many Rh-negative mothers gave birth to healthy babies. Their advice was the same as Dr. Chang's: keep taking the blood test, and watch out for the antibody ratio.

On a Saturday morning three months after we came back from Shanghai, Joe got a dreadful call from his sister Yanhua: his brother Rende had been diagnosed with stage four lung cancer! Rende had been complaining about back pain for a while. Finally a cat scan revealed tumors on the lung that had spread to other organs and bones.

Joe was visibly shaken after the phone call. I saw the same pain and agony on his face as his father and sister battled this ugly disease that eventually claimed their lives. Fifteen years ago when Joe received the call about his oldest sister's illness, we were living on Long Island, in a small dorm room on the campus of State University of New York at Stony Brook where I was pursuing my Master degree in Business and Joe was working on his Ph.D. thesis at a nearby national lab. At the time I had been in the U.S. for three years and was getting extremely homesick. At Joe's suggestion, I applied for Advance Parole that would guarantee my re-entry into America. We didn't have enough money to pay for two tickets, and Joe thought I should go see Grandma and visit his sister Meihua.

When I saw Meihua in the hospital, she appeared to be in good spirit but almost unrecognizable due to severe weight loss. Cancer had sucked up every ounce of her energy but not her desire to live. And she had so much to live for. Her older daughter had just given birth to a baby girl, and her husband who loved her dearly was at the peak of his career. We talked a little bit before she got too tired. I presented Meihu with a Bible and some pamphlets and then left with Yanhua.

"What is that little stool next to her pillow for?" I asked Yanhua.

"It was custom-made for Sister. She suffers tremendous pain when she coughs and frequently Sister coughs up a storm. With the stool, she can bend over it when she has to cough, and it gives her upper body some relief." Yanhua finished with a sigh.

Meihua's terminal illness was like a cloud over our head. Joe withdrew and hid himself in the lab working. The helplessness was what was eating him up. There was nothing Joe could do to stop where his sister was heading or even taking away her physical suffering. When we prayed together for Meihua, Joe was always wordless. I had a hard time with his withdrawal and the distance between us. We started to grow apart.

Meihua passed away in less than a year. Because of our student visa status and financial constraint, Joe didn't go back to Shanghai to attend the funeral and say his final 'goodbye' to his beloved sister who was fourteen years older and often times took care of him like a mother.

After hearing the horrible news about Rende, Joe retreated to the bedroom. I followed and lied on the bed next to him. Joe's face was tight and closed. Tears welled up in his eyes. I turned to hold him and he began crying in my arms.

"I need to go see him. I'll do whatever I can to help."

"Yes, you should go, as soon as possible. Let's find the next available flight."

After dinner, Joe and I took a long walk holding each other's hands. We talked about his dad, his sister, Rende, and lung cancer. Even though Rende had just quit smoking, his dad and sister never smoked. Joe was cautiously optimistic this time. He Googled all afternoon and found a new FDR-approved chemotherapy drug, Traceva, that targeted a specific protein within the cancer cells and could stop them from growing. It could treat a specific type of non-small cell lung cancer no matter what stage. He was going to have his brother give it a try. One of his college classmates ran one of the largest clinical trial networks in China. Joe had emailed him seeking advice on what kind of new trial drugs were out there that Rende might benefit from.

On Monday, my beloved Joe got on a plane and flew to Shanghai. He hired a taxi to get to Yanhua's, left his luggage there and went straight to the hospital. When I called, he told me he had talked to the hospital director about Rende's treatment plans. Rende would receive both chemo and radiation therapies. Traceva was not offered in China yet, but the director said he could obtain them through his personal source. It would cost fifty-five U.S. dollars a pill. Joe asked him to get seven. Supposedly if it worked, the result would be immediate and Rende would have to take it daily for the rest of his life. Joe then handed the phone to his brother.

"How are you doing, bro?" I asked, trying to sound as calm as I possibly could.

"Hongwei, I am OK. I'll be strong and fight this thing. I won't give up!"

"I have no doubt you will. We're going to do whatever it takes to help. I have our whole church praying for you."

"Thank you so much," his voice trembled.

*God, please let Rende live. He is only fifty-one. Please spare his life the same way you spared mine!*

Joe sent our Bible study group and me daily updates on Rende's condition. Joe told us he spent most of the day in the hospital taking care of his brother, talking to the doctors, reading the Bible to him, and listening to music with him. Since cancer had spread to Rende's bones, the pain was unbearable. Rende described the pain as so excruciating that it made him want to jump off a building.

Rende's wife Jin grew desperate. She threw their life savings on anything others thought might cure cancer. Some salesmen even got into the hospital wards selling herbs and other stuff, claiming they were highly effective. Jin bought them too and begged Rende to take them and get better. Joe got frustrated and tried to persuade her to stick with the treatment plan: chemo, radiation, and Traceva if chemo failed to shrink the tumors.

Rev. Zhong happened to be in Shanghai the same week Joe was there. He visited Rende in the hospital, and Rende accepted Jesus Christ as his personal Savior. When Joe reported the hospital baptism in his email, everyone rejoiced!

A few weeks after Joe got back to Chicago, it became obvious that the chemotherapy wasn't effective. As a last resort, Joe asked his brother to try Traceva. After taking the first pill, Rende got visibly better. His appetite improved, and he was even able to get up and move around a little. We were all very encouraged. Joe and I earnestly hoped that Traceva would do the magic and save his life. We eagerly waited to see if the improvement would stick.

At week eighteen of my pregnancy, Dr. Chang referred me to Dr. Graham, a fetal medicine specialist. In addition to giving me advice on the antibody concern, he was to perform a level two ultrasound that provided very detailed 3-D moving images of the fetus. It was amazing! We saw a clear profile of our baby: closed eyes, little nose, little mouth, and the tiny little fingers. Then the baby turned and I thought I saw something that resembled a male organ.

"Is it a boy?" I wondered aloud.

"Ya think?" Dr. Graham laughed. "I never say one hundred percent, but it looks like a boy to me."

I turned to Joe. He was grinning from ear to ear, and his eyes turned into the shape of the crescent moon.

Dr. Graham sat us down after the ultrasound. He was a dark-skinned, middle-aged man who wore black amber classic pantoshaped glasses. When he started talking, he sounded knowledgeable and intelligent.

"The ultrasound shows that the fetus is about seven ounces and five and a half inches, the size of a sweet potato. All the organs appear to be developing normally. From the speed of the blood pumping into the brain, we can estimate the odds of Down syndrome." He showed us a chart and did some calculation. "It's one to one thousand." It sounded much better than the odds estimated for women of my age group: one to one hundred and seventy-five.

"As for the antibodies," he continued, "we'll have to keep a close eye on the blood test results. Right now your antibody ratio is one to two. It goes up exponentially. If it ever reaches one to thirty-two, I'll have to see you every week. Worst comes worst, I can perform blood transfusion to the fetus when he is still in your womb."

"I hope it will never come to that," I said.

"It probably won't be necessary, but I want you to know the worst scenario."

I felt quite positive upon leaving Dr. Graham's office. The baby was going to live no matter what! Joe commented that our baby's profile resembled his. I laughed. But yes, it would be wonderful to have a baby boy who looked just like his daddy.

As the new life in my womb grew in leaps and bounds, Rende's life was withering away. Traceva didn't work on Rende. Joe's classmate sent the newest medicine from Beijing to Shanghai by air, but nothing happened either. Rende's condition worsened daily. Now he depended heavily on morphine and became increasingly dopey and unresponsive.

Joe was torn between the joy of having a son of his own and the grief of losing his dear brother to cancer. He grew quieter. His daily phone call to his brother became every other day, a couple of times a week, once a week, and then I had to remind him to call. "Honey, shouldn't you call Rende and see how he is doing?"

"He is always sleeping. I don't really get to talk to him anymore, plus what am I going to say? He is looking up to me to save him. I have tried everything. I don't know what to do anymore." Joe looked defeated.

Joe wanted to save his brother's life, not just his soul.

\*

Overcoming many hurdles, Living Water's new church building ministry was finally taking off. The congregation had approved the $4.5M budget and the church building committee was working feverishly to prepare all the paperwork required by the city counsel for the public hearing. The church building deacon Kurt had only been on the job for six months, but he and his wife were going to move to California, and he recommended me to fill that role.

"You got to be kidding. I know nothing about building a house, let alone a church," I told him.

"There is a lot of knowledge in the building committee. What we need is not expertise, but someone who can get the team members to work together and serve as a liaison between the committee and the Board of Deacons."

"There has to be someone else who can do this. I am having a baby!"

"There really is no one else. You are the one!"

Whenever something was presented to me as a challenge and I was called to do it, it would excite me.

"Okay, OK, I'll think about it," I mumbled.

Joe and I discussed it. He was not too thrilled about me taking on that kind of commitment for the next three years.

"Are you sure you want to do this? We're having a baby, and that's a huge commitment by itself."

"Hopefully I won't need to get into the nitty-gritty of the building process. Kurt said my main responsibilities were to get people to work together and the whole church to support the ministry. It's kind of acting like a coordinator. I think I am pretty good at that. Don't you?" I winked at him.

"Can any of the guys do this? How about Scott? He is very well liked. I am sure he can get the church united. Why do they have to ask you all the time?"

"Scott has made commitments to other ministries that are very important. They sort of think that I am the only one who can do this job." I looked at him adoringly.

"It's not that no one else can do it, but nobody else wants to do it!"

"So if I take this position, you will help me all the way like you always do because you love me, right?"

"If I don't help you, who will?" He smiled at me, acting annoyed.

Joe had been married to me long enough to know that once something got stuck in my head, it would be hard to change my mind.

Rev. Zhong and the BOD chair paid us a home visit in November, and I officially accepted the candidacy. As they put it, the church was entering uncharted water, and we would have to learn as we went. Joe acted supportive as he always did. Kurt had conveniently forgotten to mention that as the church building deacon, I would also have to take over Scott's responsibility of raising funds for the new building since other ministries bogged him down. I had my work cut out for me!

In January of 2006, with a big belly and Joe by my side, I swore in with the rest of the newly elected deacons in front of the congregation.

Meanwhile I kept an eye on my antibody level. It fluctuated during the course of my pregnancy, and my nerve fluctuated with it. News from home about Rende became more and more dismal: he was not able to keep anything down, and he was swollen because he could not urinate as cancer was attacking other parts of his body. I could feel Joe's heartache at the prospect of losing another of his siblings.

Doctor Chang recommended induced labor due to the high-risk nature of my pregnancy. I was not too crazy about the idea. I preferred to let Jacob choose his own birthday. But she managed to convince me that it was the best for the baby. My original due date was April the 13th and Doctor Chang scheduled for Jacob to be induced on April the 5th. I gave birth to both Jane and Michelle ahead of their due dates and I was hoping Jake would arrive earlier as well without any induction.

Joe and I did a lot of walking the weekend before Wednesday, April the 5th, but there wasn't any sign of contractions. I went to bed on Tuesday with a dull tummy ache. I thought it was constipation and somehow managed to have a good night sleep. The next morning, the cable guy came to hook up the new TV in our bedroom. My tummy ache got a little worse, but it didn't stop me from getting things done before heading to the hospital. Joe and I got into the car shortly after lunch and the pain became more pronounced.

Joe advised me to time the pain. I looked at my watch: 2:31 pm.

"Oh, here it comes again." The time was 2:36 pm.

"Maybe you don't need to be induced after all." Joe winked at me.

"Maybe not! Little Jacob knows what mama wants. I love this boy!"

As we entered the maternity ward the nurse shouted, "Four-five-six!"

"What does 'four-five-six' mean?" Joe asked her.

"All babies born today have the birthday April 5th, 2006, four-five-six."

"Oh, interesting." We smiled at each other.

We were placed in a comfortable room that looked a lot like an emergency room, just a little bigger, with a bed, a couch, a couple of monitors, and some medical equipment. I thought I was going to be induced there and then moved to the operation room for delivery. I ended up having Jake right there in that cozy and homey room.

A very cheerful nurse came in. Her black hair was in a ponytail, and she was pretty like a doll. She told us she had four kids. I liked her instantly. She would understand what I was about to go through.

"You look like you are ready to have this baby." She looked at my baby bump and smiled.

"I might be in labor already. Please check first," I informed her.

"Okay. Let's take a look," she declared excitedly after a couple of minutes of stillness. "Oh my, oh my! You are certainly in labor! As a matter of fact, you are already seven centimeters dilated. Let me call you doctor."

Dr. Chang was in her office with a few more patients to see for the day. She instructed the nurse to have me stay put. Dr. Chang was afraid the baby would just pop out since this was my third.

There wasn't really much to do. Joe and I just stayed in the room and waited. The nurse came back a few times to check the progress of my dilation and the contraction frequency.

"Wow, that's a big one!" She glanced at the monitor and then turned to me. "Do you need anything for the pain?"

"No, it's not that bad. I'm OK."

Around seven o'clock that evening, the contractions became more frequent and intense, the natural force had kicked in with all its power and glory to separate the baby from his mother's womb.

"Now I can use something to ease the pain," I made a request to the nurse.

"Sorry, but it's too late. Whatever I give you now will go into the baby's blood stream which may cause harm."

*No problem. I'll just have to tough it out. This is good pain compared to the ectopic pain. I can take it!*

Dr. Chang finally arrived around 7:30. She was ready for a quick delivery.

"Linda, give me a few big pushes. Let's get this baby out."

I arched my body and pushed as hard as I could a few times. Nothing happened.

"Push harder, OK? I don't want to cut you if I don't have to."

When I had Jane and Michelle, the male obstetricians were quick to make vaginal cut in order to make room for the baby's head to come out. Dr. Chang was more into getting it done naturally. Little Jacob just didn't seem to want to come out yet.

"Let's give it one more try. If it doesn't happen this time, I'll have to—I really don't want to do that."

I got into position again and pushed with every ounce of energy left in me.

Here came our precious baby boy! He had his right little hand rested on his temple, and his elbow blocked the way out. That was why I had such a hard time pushing him out. *Funny little guy, he is already a thinker in mommy's tummy!*

I took Jacob from the nurse with trembling hands and looked at him with such pride and joy. He looked perfect to me. Joe held both of us in his arms and whispered, "He is so handsome. I love you. I'm so proud of you!" I was laughing and crying at the same time.

\*

Repeatedly I prayed for a miracle. I had heard and read about the wonderful work God was doing in the rural areas of China. In some cases, God would miraculously heal someone with a terminal disease, and as a result, the whole village became believers. I pleaded with God to cure Rende so that our seventy or so families and relatives would be saved as well. But God had a different plan.

On March 24th, less than two weeks before Jacob was born, Rende passed away in the hospital peacefully, leaving behind his wife and twenty-three-year-old daughter. Joe knew this was imminent and was mentally prepared for it. When the news came, he retreated to the bedroom and closed the door. About half an hour later, Joe reemerged looking exhausted but not crushed.

I gave him a big hug. "Are you going to be OK, baby?"

"I'll be alright. Life comes and life goes, there is nothing anyone can do about that. Now I can't wait to welcome little Jacob to this world." He put his hands on my big belly and smiled a tired smile.

A few days after we brought Jacob home, I heard Joe screaming through the baby monitor. "He peed, he peed!"

I ran upstairs and saw Joe holding Jake's pee in his palms, still laughing.

We had moved into a newer and bigger house before I got pregnant. The master bedroom was on the first floor and the other bedrooms on the second. Had we known there was going to be another baby, we probably would have had bought a house with a different layout since going up and down at night to care for an infant was quite an exercise. Normally Joe fell asleep quickly and could sleep through a thunderstorm. But every time Jake cried at night, he would jump up like a jack-in-the-box.

"Is he hungry again?" I groaned, half asleep.

"Go back to sleep. I'll go feed him."

"He cries really loud for such a little baby."

"I love it!"

"Even at night?"

"Yes, the sound of the cry symbolizes life, the existence of a brand new life in this house, and I love it!"

Joe had told me that caring for Jake was entirely different from caring for his brother in the hospital. With a new life comes new hope and new dreams. But with Rende, that hope dimmed a little every day as his condition worsened. It was also gut wrenching to watch Rende go through that kind of pain.

Zuo Yuezi (sitting out the month) is one of the ancient Chinese traditions for new mothers. Within thirty days after giving birth, the new mother is supposed to spend all of her time indoors, much of it in bed. She is prohibited from bathing, washing her hair, or brushing her teeth. The food regimen of *zuo yue zi* is unbelievably complex. I didn't follow the tradition after giving birth to Jane and Michelle, but I did manage to stay indoors for a couple of weeks. Now with three kids, things got even crazier. My recovery was speedier this time because of the complete natural birth, and so I started taking Jane and Michelle to school in the morning just a few days after. Who could have the heart to wake up Joe since he had been up numerous times at night to feed Jake and he was sound asleep when the girls were ready for school? I also had to go to the supermarket to restock the refrigerator. A couple of older women from church saw me in the store.

When I got home, Joe said that some woman had called and scolded him harshly for not keeping me at home. She disapproved of the way I was running around. I was speechless. Later I tried to go to the store on Friday evening or Sunday morning when everyone else was in church.

Joe hardly had time to dwell on the loss of his brother. He didn't go to the funeral because it was so close to my due date, so he wrote a eulogy to his brother and asked Yanhua to read it on his behalf. Joe turned the pain of loss to a rigorous effort at gaining understanding of the gene mutation process that caused cancer. He started bringing lots of books home from the library and researching information online. The answers he was going to find weren't anything either of us would have ever expected.

# Betrayal

One of the main reasons I gravitated to Christian faith and the church community was the value it placed on family. For someone raised in a disjointed home full of bitterness, anger, and conflicts, family is near and dear to my heart.

To strengthen family relationship and witness God's love in Christian families, Rev. Zhong and I came up with the idea to host an annual vow renewal ceremony so that couples got a chance to exchange vows in front of God, families, and friends. It also gave the ladies the long-waited opportunity to wear wedding gowns since white gown was not popular in the eighties when people of my generation got married in China. I volunteered to be the ceremony coordinator. The scope of my job was to not only organize the event but also persuade mostly reluctant husbands to walk down the aisle with their wives.

"You look beautiful together. Turn to each other a little bit more. Yes, that's perfect!" I smiled at the couple posing for pictures on the lawn outside the Chinese Christian Church.

It was Living Water Church's fourth vow renewal ceremony. This time five couples participated. They were all married in China before becoming Christians. Living Water used to be a branch church of Chinese Christian Church. Due to the rapid Asian population growth in Naperville, in 2000, thirty-five families from Chinese Christian Church started a branch in Naperville by renting the facility of a local junior high school. Living Water soon outgrew its mother church. The church eventually broke into two.

The whole church was in a festive mood that day. The auditorium was fully decorated. A large silk ivory rose wreath was placed over the entrance door, with rose garlands extended from the wreath and hung over the sides of the doorframe. The auditorium had a seating capacity of 150. Each of the eight rows of pews was decorated on the side of the center aisle with flower bouquet and ivory tulle swaging freely in between the pews. Two candle stands stood gracefully on both side of the podium, each with twelve candleholders covered by flowers and tulles. A fresh white rose bouquet was set on a long table under the podium.

Volunteer makeup artists used their talent to make the brides look beautiful. A couple of semi-professional photographers got all their gear out to take pictures of the couples. Lunch was delivered by a group of volunteer sisters for the vow-renewing couples and their families. Another group of coworkers prepared fruits, snacks, and desserts for the reception after the ceremony.

It was a fun and exciting day, but pressure could be high at times. I had to make sure that everything flowed smoothly especially that each couple followed the makeup and photo session schedules so that everyone was ready for the afternoon ceremony. "Please look at the schedule I just passed out, and follow it at all cost. Because if you don't, I am going to come after you like a mad woman," I reminded every couple beforehand, half-jokingly.

But almost every year, someone would disrupt the schedule and cause a spiral impact on everyone else. Today Mei and her husband strolled in as if they were the spectators instead of the participants. Her hair was not done, and she wore a cap!

I gasped, "Mei, your makeup session starts in ten minutes. You're supposed to get your hair done at home."

"Really? I thought someone here was going to do my hair."

She opted out of having a professional hairdresser from church put her hair up. But this was not the time to argue or to really act like a mad woman. I looked around. Everyone was busy, so I sat her down and started combing and braiding her long beautiful hair. I was not good at this kind of stuff, but her headpiece and would cover the flaws of my work. And the important thing was I brought us back on schedule.

After lunch, all couples and their families gathered outside the church for group pictures. I had learned from past experience that it was not possible to get everyone at the same spot at one time no matter how hard I tried, and so as long as all the brides and grooms were present, it was good to go. Then the five brides posed for pictures under a big willow tree in the front lawn. It was a picture perfect late summer day, and the women looked gorgeous, like angels descending from heaven. Their veils danced gracefully in the gentle breeze, and they smiled so happily for the camera. All the stress we went through in the morning to get them ready paid off at that moment.

According to the schedule, at 1:45 all were expected to line up outside the auditorium. Two teenagers led the line holding the long candle lighters, followed by six flower girls and two ring bearers, with the brides and grooms at the end of the line. I did a headcount and realized a flower girl was missing. A few of my helpers went looking for her and ended up finding her in one of the classrooms playing with the toys. She was brought back in line. All these adorable kids were children of the vow-renewing couples.

At two o'clock, the elegant tune of "Two Rings," played by the pianist and violinist, resounded throughout the church building. The teens walked slowly down the aisle, got up the stage, and lit up the candle one by one. There was always a couple that flickered and then went out, followed by a kind chuckle from the audience. Then the cute flower girls started walking in pairs, sprinkling the rose peddles along the central aisle. They smiled and waved to their friends in the audience. The boys looked more serious and nervous each holding a white ring pillow. Finally, Rev. Zhong gave a brief introduction of every couple as they made their grand entrance into the auditorium, and each bride walked down the aisle with her husband. Everyone stood up, admiring the stunning brides, the handsome grooms, and their beautiful children. I got to sit down and take a sigh of relief at that point, waiting for the best part of the ceremony: the family slideshows and the vow exchanges.

Jack and Victoria had been married for twenty-six years. Jack was six feet tall with a flat top haircut. He looked like a tough guy. "I stand today in front our family, our friends, and you, Victoria, to reaffirm my marriage vows. I will continue to love you, take care of you and protect you the same way Christ loves his church. By the grace of God, I desire to grow with you, serving Him, and building a Christ-centered home. In the days ahead, for better for worse, for richer or poorer, in sickness and in health, I will love you forever. The sea may run dry and the rocks may crumble, but my heart will always remain in love with you. May the Lord help me keep my vow!" his voice trembled. Suddenly, he cried like a baby and could barely continue on. His wife's eyes sparkled with tears and soon the whole congregation was crying. I also noticed Jack's grownup son and his girlfriend held hands and looked at each other lovingly.

My eyes grew moist. Joe and I renewed our vows three years ago on the same Labor Day weekend. Joe froze a few times when he couldn't remember parts of his vow, which rocked the whole auditorium with laugher. He really tried hard to get it right, even reciting it in his dream the night before. I stood opposite him, finding it hard to believe that the normally eloquent Joe could get so nervous and tongue-tied. But I knew every word he managed to get out, he meant.

At the time of the ceremony, we had no idea that our resolution to keep the vows would be put to test immediately. Within a couple of months, Joe lost his job and embarked on a trying journey to start his own business. In the beginning, he had big dreams and wanted to make a quick success by setting his foot in the high tech industry. Soon it was obvious that the high return also meant high risk and bigger investment. He then tried to start a consulting firm, but companies were cutting back, and it would take years to build clientele. We even sold wedding gowns imported from China on eBay. In the beginning, business was decent, but soon too many people entered the crowded selling space, and the profit margin eroded.

Ever since I knew Joe, he had been the shoulder for me to lean on. But during those eighteen months, it was the first time I felt he needed me more than ever before. I got through those uncertain and at times stressful days by reminding myself of the vows I made and by holding onto God's word. Joe got upset once when I tried to give him unsolicited advice on where to take his business. I walked away disheartened because of his unwillingness to take my constructive criticism. He didn't come to the bedroom that evening. Lying in bed I watched our vow renew tape one more time and then paced back and forth, torn between what I wanted to do and what I ought to do. Finally I went to the study and found him sleeping on the floor. He turned his back to me when I switched on the light. The room was blanketed with a thick silence that seemed impossible to penetrate. Then hearing my own voice surprised me.

"I—I only meant to give you some suggestions, but they probably didn't come through the right way. I am sorry for upsetting you. Will you come to the room and sleep on the bed?" A sense of freedom dawned on me immediately. I extended my hand, and he took it. That was the first time I had ever said sorry to Joe before he apologized first.

Witnessing these couples in front of me strengthening their union in such a meaningful way simply brought joy and gratefulness to my heart. For a while life was extremely hectic but fulfilled. I felt blessed to be able to serve God in a growing church community, to have a husband who supported me, two beautiful girls who still enjoyed hanging around with mom, and little Jacob who made our lives busier but complete.

Sitting in a wooden rocking chair with baby blue back and seat cushions bought when Jane with born and with Jacob in my arms, I studied his chubby face with great interest. He was trying to talk to me by making baby noises. A year ago Joe and I were not sure about having another baby, now I could hardly imagine our life without little Jacob. Jacob was going to be much more than a bundle of joy; he was going to lighten up the lonely and agonizing journey ahead of me.

\*

The Naperville city council granted Living Water Church a building permit in January 2006. But we had to provide many details and modifications to the building design before reaching the annexation agreement with the council. A lot of the church members were present at the annexation hearing in October of that year. After waiting patiently for almost three hours for the council to go through all the other items on the agenda, they approved our case with one hundred percent votes in less than five minutes.

"The city of Naperville welcomes Living Water Church to our community!" Mayor Pradel opened his arms and announced enthusiastically. The mayor is short and energetic. His big belly, broad smile, and cheerful demeanor all make him resemble Santa Clause without the red suit and white beard.

In preparation for the groundbreaking ceremony in late October, a canopy was put up on the lawn that served as the center stage and rows of chairs were lined up in front of it. Even though it was an unusually chilly and windy day for October, our hearts were filled with joy, excitement, and a deep sense of pride. We, as an Asian church, had been wandering in the desert for eight years. Living Water was required to renew the lease with the junior high school on an annual basis. They threatened to terminate the lease almost every year. Even though the school district welcomed the extra income, the teachers were very unhappy about having our kids in their classrooms on weekends. It was like walking on egg shells most of the time.

Mayor Pradel and one of the councilmen attended our groundbreaking ceremony. We sang, danced to the music, and gave thanks to God. Rev. Zhong outlined Living Water's vision to serve God, spread the Gospel, and serve the community. The mayor knew how to work the crowd. After his speech, we were all fired up, looking into a near future when the old houses on the site would be torn down and a brand new church built by a group of Asians would emerge in its place. It would be our spiritual home away from home. The congregation was given the impression that the new church would be built in about a year.

Our architect, Rick, was a super nice guy. He looked like my Uncle Mao Mao: thin, soft-spoken, and enormously patient although he had a reputation for not finishing the job on time. We knew that when we hired him to finish the blueprint for the new building. He only asked for a fraction of what a consulting company would have charged. To save more money, we asked him to stay on as the construction manager. Rick had to work on another unfinished project while managing the construction of our new church. He wasn't able to be on site as much as we needed him. So we hired a full-time project manager, Ruth, to monitor the progress and assist Rick. Ruth was middle-aged with black curly shoulder-length hair that was meticulously styled. Ruth was always smiling and a devoted church volunteer who served as the principal of the children's Sunday school for many years. In order to inspire the Sunday school teachers to get well prepared for their classes, I once heard Ruth telling them that she herself had spent twenty hours preparing for one lesson. Ruth's husband, Luke, used to be a key member of the building committee but later quit. Luke and Rick had been long-time friends. We felt comfortable that with the support from her husband, her friendship with Rick, and the closeness of her residence to the new building, she could keep a close eye on the contractors while maintaining open communications with Rick.

I became the liaison between BOD and the building committee and the face of the new building ministry. It was a challenging job because of a very tight budget, the unrealistic expectations all around, and a strained relationship between BOD and the building committee. Maybe Joe was right. It was not that nobody could do this job, but nobody wanted to do it.

In spite of all the craziness, Joe and I managed to find time to be with each other and with Jake. We enjoyed taking a walk together after dinner. Joe always teased that I walked as if I were in a hurry to get somewhere. I tried to slow down. Sometimes I would go ahead of the stroller and suddenly turn around to surprise Jake. He thought it was the funniest thing and would giggle like crazy. Watching Joe going down the slide with Jake in the park was another one of my favorite things to do.

From time to time I would bring my struggles home and share with Joe the sticky issues related to the new church building. He would give me advice and help me see things more objectively. I could always count on Joe's support. He was as reliable and predictable as Newton's laws of physics.

*

My reliable and predictable Joe began to change in small but noticeable ways. He was still affectionate but grew distant. In our weekly Bible study fellowship, instead of discussing straightforward questions, he was joking about almost everything.

"Honey, are you OK? Do you want to talk about anything?" I probed every once in a while.

"I'm fine. Why are you asking?"

"It's like you can't be serious about anything ..."

"I just wanted to loosen the atmosphere. It was getting boring. Really, I am fine," he assured me.

"OK. I am always here if you need to talk, OK?"

"I know, baby."

Shortly after Jake turned one, the cumulative change in him became alarming. One night Jake went to sleep early and Joe was in bed reading. I sat beside him.

"Honey, you've changed in the past year. Your attitude towards God and the church, I can't really pinpoint it, but I need to know what's going on there." I pointed at his head.

"So you've noticed." He cleared his throat. "I—I didn't want to bother you. You have been so busy taking care of our home, Jake, your job, and all the church work. I didn't want to weigh you down or distract you."

"Can you just get to the point instead of going round and round?"

"Okay, I'll tell you. But promise you won't be mad. OK?"

"I'll try not to." I fixed my eyes on him.

"After Rende passed away, I started to think hard. Is there really eternal life? What is death? What is pain? I've read a lot about gene mutation, and it led me to study Darwin's evolution theories. The church always preaches evolution is false because God created everything. I am not in the field of biology, so I've never really looked into it. But the more I read about it, the more I am convinced that it is not false. The scientific evidence is plenty and solid. The Biblical version of creation is questionable."

"S-s-s-o what are you saying?" I was stunned.

"That the Judaism God described in the Bible may not exist."

"No, He has to exist! God saved me. He gave us an abundant new life. He gave us Jacob. He made our lives meaningful. How could you say that? You have experienced God just like I have!" I started to physically move away from him.

He pulled me closer and held me. "Baby, listen. I don't draw these conclusions lightly. I have struggled for almost a year, but I am afraid they are true!"

"It can't be true. I talk to God every day, and he talks to me. He is real, and I know it!" Joe still had me in his arms, but I was drifting away emotionally.

"That's why I have also been studying how our brain works. Our brain can fool us into believing things that are not real."

"Your brain may fool you, but mine doesn't fool me." I freed myself from his hold, walked into the bathroom and closed the door.

I sat on the brim of the Sanibel whirlpool tub feeling betrayed, angry, confused, and lost. I was cheated. Joe had hidden a secret from me for over a year. We were supposed to be transparent with each other. One of the things I had feared the most in life was sitting in a doctor's office and being told Joe had stage IV lung cancer. But he was healthy. Nobody was not going to die. But something just died. I buried my face in my hands and cried.

"Baby, are you OK in there? Can we talk more?" Joe knocked on the door.

"No, I want to be alone."

He walked back to bed. And my thoughts took me back to years ago when we first met.

Joe and I were both at my uncle and his sister's wedding banquet, but there were a lot of people there so didn't meet each other. Yanhua was very proud of his brother and talked about him constantly. She told us that he had been accepted into the graduate program at Shanghai Jiao Tong University. I wanted to meet her brother who was going to be a graduate student at my dream university. For some reason, I imagined Joe to be an old guy since I was only a high school freshman at the time, anyone over twenty was old to me, and his Chinese name Zhongde, which meant loyalty and virtue, made him sound old as well.

One day Yanhua said that his brother was coming to Aunt's place to visit. I came home from school after rehearsing for a large-scaled performance for a major sports event in Shanghai. I wore a white gymnastic suit with bright pink trim. My hair was in a ponytail on the top of my head. I looked like a little gymnast except that my body was not flexible enough to do any of the moves they could do. I was skinny and petite like a bean sprout.

"Is Zhongde here yet?" I wondered loudly as I came in the door.

A young man in his early twenties sitting on our willow armchair with his back towards the door turned around and looked at me. He wore a gray modern Chinese tunic suit, gold-framed thick eyeglasses, and with a book in his hand. He had the appearance of a typical diligent Chinese scholar, quite handsome, too.

*He'll make a good husband for me someday.* I surprised myself with that thought.

"This is Uncle Zhongde. Where are your manners, young lady?" Grandma corrected me.

"Oh, hi, hello, Uncle Zhongde. How are you?" I giggled.

When he smiled, his eyes smiled too. I fell in love.

Joe majored in physics. Physics was my least favorite subject. It never made sense to me. I asked him to be my tutor because a better test score on physics could only improve my chance to be accepted by Jiao Tong University.

I started going to Jiao Tong University every weekend bringing with me all the physics problems I didn't want to solve. Joe would solve them one by one and explain to me in detail the methodology and theories used. I would listen quietly without giving him clear indication as to whether I got it or not. He would go on and on until he thought I understood. I loved spending time with him, and my weekly tutoring session soon became the highlight of my week.

One Saturday I arrived at his dorm in the torrential rain. He looked anxious. "I was afraid you were not going to show up today."

"Why? I said I was to come."

"Look at you. You are soaking wet. You must be hungry too. Let's go to the cafeteria and get something to eat."

Joe ordered extra food and was particularly sweet and somewhat nervous that day.

I normally took the bus home after the tutoring session, but Joe offered to walk me home in the rain. It would take more than an hour. We walked silently under the same umbrella. I had a feeling something was about to happen.

"I'd like to tell you a story. Do you want to hear it?" Joe broke the silence, clearing his throat.

"I'd love to hear it," I replied quietly.

"Once there was a little boy who lived with his grandparents in Pu Dong. His parents came to see him and his brother on weekends. On a cold sunny winter day when he was about five, he went out to play by himself. He walked on the lake that was frozen. Soon he started running and jumping and was having so much fun. Suddenly the ice broke and he dropped into the freezing water. He tried frantically to pull himself out. He succeeded. The little boy ran as fast as his little legs could carry him back home.

He had a high fever for a few days and later developed severe bronchitis and eczema. His parents took him back to Shanghai. Many nights he couldn't breathe, and they had to take him to the hospital, sometimes more than once in a single night. He felt guilty for being such a burden to his mom and dad. They had eight kids and had to work hard enough for the family without him being sick all the time. He didn't go to school most of the time as a result of his poor health. During his last year in high school, the college entrance exam system was restored for the first time after the Cultural Revolution. With only a few months to prepare for the big exam, he worked hard and absorbed everything like a sponge. He passed with flying colors and got into the physics department at Jiao Tong University. He started working out in college and his respiratory problems no longer bothered him. Although he had a girlfriend from high school, she had broken up with him because she didn't want to be limited …"

Joe paused, took a deep breath and then continued. "This young man met a very young girl not too long ago. He liked her at first sight. She is beautiful and different from anyone he has ever met. He didn't imagine anything could happen between them because she was very young. But his sister has hinted to him that the girl likes him too. He really loves her. Do you think the girl might have feelings for him too?"

Listening attentively without interrupting him even once, I blushed scarlet at his question, but responded without hesitation, "She loves him too."

Joe beamed. The next thing I knew he pressed a kiss on my forehead. My very first kiss! It sent a tickling sensation up and down my spine. With my heart racing like a wild horse, I forgot to watch where I was going in the rain and stepped into a puddle and the water splashed all over me. We looked at each other and burst into laughter. Joe and I huddled closer under the umbrella with his arm wrapped around my shoulder and continued walking and talking. Joe did most of the talking as usual. My pants were wet up to my knees when I got home, but I felt warm and fuzzy inside. It was sweet to be in love!

Joe took it upon himself to love me and protect me from that day on. He treated me like a precious gem, something priceless to him. I admired and adored him.

I belonged to a computer club at the time. There was a Youths Creation and Convention Contest in Shanghai. The club instructor required us to enter the contest, and he came up with an invention idea for each of us. Mine was to use the microphone volume meter on an analogue tape recorder to record the street noise level. He did the whole creation and invention part, and all I had to do was walk with the tape recorder on the street and write down the noise level numbers on a sheet. The judge panel liked his invention, and I was asked to go in front of them and explain how I came up with the idea and made it work. Needless to say it was not my idea, and I had no clue. So Joe prepped me for it with a list of possible questions and answers. I did well, only missed one very detailed technical question. They awarded me with the second prize!

Joe always carried in his pocket my favorite snack. He would offer it to me whenever I got frustrated with the stupid physics assignments. He became the father I had never had, a big brother, and a lover. He was everything to me! We had our share of problems and struggles especially after I entered college. But I was convinced from day one that we were meant for each other and together we would build the loving home that I had been yearning for. *But this is different. We have built our home on God's word. I have lived and breathed for God the past ten years. How are we going to deal with this crisis?*

I slid down to the tile floor and put my head on the side of the tub. There were no stars visible from the skylight window, a tiny crack in the ceiling. I wondered, if left alone, how long it would take for this crack to become a big whole in our roof. *My perfect marriage and life now have a crack!*

\*

Joe's effort to start his own business during his eighteen-month unemployment didn't turn futile. His online business selling small office equipment did eventually take off. Our best-selling product was a manual paper cutter that could cut three hundred sheets of paper with one stroke. Joe put a lot of effort into product design and brand development. He also registered a trademark for the cutters. Orders kept coming in, and business was good for a while.

Then we had a copycat, someone who sold the paper cutters with the exact same appearance, same description, but at a lower price. Upon close inspection, we realized that Mr. Copycat had directly copied product photos from our listings to his. We reported it to eBay, and his listing was suspended. A few days later he came up with his own photos and somehow got re-listed. Mr. Copycat's company was registered in Nevada under a phony name, with a mailbox address in Las Vegas and operated via a UPS store mailbox address in Naperville. Could this be someone we knew? We had made it no secret that we were in the paper cutter business. Living Water had one of our cutters in the secretary's office and our home address was listed on our company's website for a short period of time.

Numerous customers contacted us claiming they had problems with our products that turned out to be his. Since we both shipped from Naperville, some assumed we were affiliated. It had become a big headache. Joe changed the color of the cutters from gray to black and added some enhanced features. Within a couple of months, Copycat did the same thing. And then he filed IP infringement complaints to eBay claiming we had copied him. It took Joe a couple of weeks to explain and provide evidence that we had started selling paper cutters more than a year before he did. It became an online war! Going through the legal process would be expensive and messy. Who was this sneaky guy constantly stealing Joe's ideas and disrupting our business?

\*

The new church building was off to a rough start. The building committee realized before real ground breaking that the budget had to be increased from $4.5M to $5.6M based on actual quotes from potential contractors.

I proposed the new budget to BOD based on two factors 1) $4.5M was a rough estimate from years ago, 2) by digging out the full basement instead of half, we would increase the building square footage by about twenty percent.

"So the building committee is not going to come back and ask for more money down the road?" Righteous Ryan piped up with a touch of sarcasm in his voice. Ryan was tall and skinny with a deep, resonating voice. He often laughed unexpectedly when speaking and looked around the room to solicit support. Joe and I had been friends with Ryan and his wife for many years, but there was something about Ryan that caused me to want to be on guard.

"N-n-o-o," I replied with as much confidence as I could gather.

Mark the Doubtful expressed his doubts as he always did about how we were going to pay for our expensive new church. Eric the Critic criticized the building committee for not knowing what they were doing. "This is a twenty-five percent increase. They should have known that way earlier instead of bringing it up now, right before the construction." Stanley the Steward commented that good stewardship meant being prudent and careful about how we spent God's money.

Biting my tongue, I reckoned that everyone in the room should have known that it wasn't possible to build 40,000 plus square foot church building with a modern 550-seat theater-style auditorium, a gym, a library, a conference room, a staff office section, and more than two dozen classrooms with $4.5M. After all, those who wanted to voice their opinions had spoken, most board members agreed that this was a reasonable increase and gave the green light.

In February, the revised budget was presented to the congregation. We had set up a church building fund, and the congregation had been making donations towards it. The good news was that due to the schedule delay and the growth of the building fund, we wouldn't have to borrow more money from the bank even with the bigger budget. The new budget passed the congregational vote at the end of February, and construction finally started in April of 2007.

The challenge about our new building was that nothing ever stayed the same. In my simple mind, we had the drawings of the building, we knew how much things cost, and so all we had to do was line up the tasks in a logical order and get it done one by one. But in every committee meeting, we were constantly making small or big changes to the blueprint based on input from the staff or members of the congregation. Being a nice guy, Rick always accommodated our never-ending requests for modifications. Then there was the weather factor, especially in the initial stage of the construction. Under the mentality of saving every penny, we were pretty stingy towards all the contractors, and the end result was that they either didn't show up for work as promised or sent fewer people to our job when other more attractive projects came long. Things were taking much longer than expected. Winter came earlier in 2007, and we failed to install the roof before snow hit Chicago. Construction came to a halt and didn't pick up again until the spring of next year.

The pressure from BOD for repeatedly missing the milestones had become more pronounced. I was sure they didn't want to hear that the budget would have to be increased again! Even though churches were supposed to be different from corporates, when the stakes got high and millions of dollars were at risk, BOD adopted the mindset of corporate executives: show me the results and results only!

*

The relationship between Joe and me was also getting more strained. He tried to engage me in conversations on numerous occasions. The more I listened, the more confused, frustrated, and agonized I became. Once getting into something he considered himself knowledgeable about, Joe had the habit of going on and on and completely disregarding the reaction of his audience. I began to find excuses not to stick around too long. The crack was turning into a small opening.

I felt totally alone in the sense that there was nobody I could talk to about Joe's change of heart towards God and the impact on me. I was supposed to be one of those who could serve God tirelessly motivated by his love and my faith in him. I was not meant to stumble. People had put me on the pedestal. I had put myself on the pedestal. The few times I did mention it to a couple of highly spiritual sisters, God's wrath was brought up, and I was reminded of the choice between God and this world. I knelt down and cried out to God more than once. "God, show me the light. Reveal yourself to me. Make me strong in you!"

Silence.

In our church, stories about God's salvation and redemption were celebrated, but it was taboo for a mature Christian to express his growing doubts about God.

Solitude.

Our married life hadn't been always rosy. As a matter of fact, our relationship was on the verge of collapse before both of us turned and devoted ourselves to God. The past ten years had been the happiest. We lived in a triangle, with God on the top, and Joe and I at the bottom. By moving towards God together, we got closer. But now that ideal structure had been ruined, and we were moving apart as a result. Part of me wanted to run away before Joe got me sucked into this Godlessness nonsense. Part of me wanted desperately to restore the beautiful love he and I had shared. *Do I still love him now that he has become an atheist? Is it possible to make things work now that we are faced with such critical differences?*

I asked the same 'Do I still love him' question after getting into college. I took a break from Joe and explored other possibilities but then came to the realization that he was the man for me. I wanted to spend the rest of my life with him.

With Joe's help, I passed physics on the college entrance exam with a whopping sixty-seven percent. Even though our love blossomed, my physics didn't. I didn't get into Jiao Tong University either, as it wasn't even listed as one of my choices. In China, one's score on the national college entrance exam alone determined her qualification. If she failed to qualify for her first choice, her other choices wouldn't be honored in the desired sequence. She could end up in a college far away from home since it was mandatory to put down at least one choice that was in another of the country other than where she lived. My teachers thought my chance for Jiao Tong was borderline. The other college that had the major I wanted was twenty minutes away from Jiao Tong by bus. I eventually chose East China University of Science and Technology because I wanted to be safe as well as be close to Joe. It turned out that my score was good enough for Jiao Tong, but I got immediate attention at East China University. I was admitted with the highest score among the students accepted into the English of Science and Technology department along with other accomplishments such as the second prize in the Creation and Convention Contest, and the title of the Most Outstanding Students of Shanghai City. I became the leader and representative of my class and started organizing the English Club and other highly visible events on campus. I became well known in a short period of time.

Boys left love notes and sometimes-lengthy love letters in my mailbox. One morning I was running on the track field when a dark skinny boy I vaguely knew caught up with me. We ran side by side for a few minutes. He said between heavy breathing that he liked me very much and wanted me to be his girlfriend. I was caught off guard but told him I already had a boyfriend. We kept running throughout the conversation.

"But can we be friends?" he persisted.

"I-I think so." I hated to disappoint anyone. He ran ahead not totally satisfied but happy. That made me happy, too.

I told Joe about the boys and the letters. He repeated the same line over and over again like a broken recorder. "Not every guy who likes you has your best interest in his heart." Now he truly sounded like my father, and it was getting annoying.

In my sophomore year, Joe's dad got gravely ill. Surgery revealed the cancer on his lungs had spread. Joe spent most his free time in the hospital, and I was getting busier at school. One cold winter day I went to the gradate students' dorm building to distribute the club forms and met Yu who frequently attended the English Club but always stood in the back. He was thrilled that I showed up at his dorm and complimented me lavishly. Yu had unusually pale skin and a seductive smile. I didn't tell Joe about him. Yu and I started hanging out. Yu didn't mind that I had a boyfriend. He simply stated, "When you are with me, don't think about him. When you are with him, don't think about me." It was against everything I believed in, but he was charming and exciting while Joe had become boring and withdrawn.

Joe's father died of lung cancer in less than six months. I missed him so much and decided to end things with Yu.

"We should stop seeing each other," I told Yu.

"But why? I thought we were having a good time."

"Yeah, but I want to patch things up with Joe. I do love him … a lot."

"Okay, then. I'll be here if things don't work out."

Joe taught at Jiao Tong after finishing his graduate program. He was working on his course notes when I found him in his dorm. His eyes didn't smile at the sight of me walking in. He was having a hard time with his father's death.

"Hi, how are you?" I pulled a chair and sat by him.

"Okay."

After a few seconds of awkward silence, I went on, "There is something I need to tell you. I have been seeing this guy from school."

He interrupted me before I could even begin. "I won't be surprised at all if I see you walking on the street holding hands with another guy. I have been through hell the last six months. I was hoping you would be there, but you were too busy doing other things. Unless you're sure you still love me and want to marry me, we shouldn't see each other again."

I was dumbfounded. *Why is he so mean?* I stood up and ran out of the room in tears.

When I got back to my dorm, all my six roommates were sitting on their beds studying or reading quietly. The seven of us shared a small two hundred square-foot room with four bunk beds. Only one bed was vacant with our stuff piled to the ceiling. There were no heating or air conditioning systems in these dorms. In winter it could get so cold that the windows were covered with a thick layer of frost and ice which made it impossible to see through. Summer was no breeze either. The chairs and our beds could get too hot to sit on. We also had to battle the mosquitoes. The white mosquito net hung over each bed year-round looked grayish and dusty.

I burst into tears. "What am I going to do? I broke up with Yu, but Joe wouldn't talk to me. Should I get back with Yu?"

They all looked up from what they were doing. Wei, my best friend, broke the silence, "Yu already has a new girlfriend. We saw them together looking really cozy."

I felt like a fool. *Yu doesn't love anyone but himself. The sooner I forget about him the better.* I wrote Joe a letter asking for a fresh start. He accepted. We were back together, only this time Joe was a bit more reserved and elusive.

Strolling in Xujiahui one day, Joe pulled out his wallet to pay for something and a used concert tickets fell out.

"Who did you go to the concert with?" I asked him.

"Oh, it was Fey. She bought the tickets and mailed one to me."

Fey was Joe's girlfriend from high school who broke up with him. She had become a doctor. Joe's dad stayed in the hospital where she worked before he passed away.

"Why did you go with her? I'm not seeing anyone else anymore." The annoyance in my voice was obvious.

"Well, she was very good to my dad. I didn't want to hurt her feelings."

"So do you feel like you owe her something, or do you still love her?"

"She's a nice person, but we don't click. I really don't want to hurt her."

Joe explained that Fey was the first girl who ever asked him out. He was flattered in spite of the fact that Fey was not really his type. Joe didn't think girls would be interested in him due to his poor health as a youth.

I felt guilty for not being there for him when he needed me the most and dropped the topic.

On a chilly Saturday morning, Joe and I took a walk in the park. I noticed he was wearing a new maroon silk scarf.

"That looks nice. Did you get it yourself?"

"Oh that … Fey gave it to me."

I was upset and didn't say much for the rest of the morning.

"Are you OK? Is something bothering you?" Joe finally broke the silence.

"I am fine." I didn't want to reveal my internal turmoil.

"Are you upset with me and Fey?"

"Yeah. So what's going on between you two?"

Finally the whole story came out. Shortly after they performed surgery on Joe's father, the doctors informed the family that there was not much they could do and sent him home. Taking care of a stage four cancer patient at home was challenging, and Joe had to ask favors from his classmates who were in the medical field for various medical supplies. No hospital was willing to take his dad in. Joe eventually went to Fey and asked her to find a way to get his dad back in the hospital. Fey arranged everything and made it happen. She was super helpful and resourceful. She called Joe's father "Dad" in front of her colleagues and other patients. One day in December, Joe was working on a project with a couple of colleagues in the computer lab. When he got out, he was told that his brother Rende had come to look for him. His father had passed away! Joe rushed to the hospital only to find that his dad had been removed from the room. He located Fey and she took him to the morgue and pulled out his father's corpse. Joe collapsed to the floor weeping. Fey held him up, and they cried in each other's arms.

After the funeral Fey sent Joe a note along with a concert ticket. She poured out her heart to him after the concert when he walked her to the bus stop. "Breaking up with you was the biggest mistake of my life. When I was in college, I got distracted, and I wasn't sure about us."

"That's OK. I can understand," Joe tried to make it sound like it wasn't a big deal.

"Will you give me another chance? If you're willing, we can get married tomorrow and start our life together."

"I'm afraid I can't do that. Linda and I are engaged. I've given her my mother's ring. I've promised to marry her after she gets out of school."

Fey sobbed.

"I think it's time for me to have a face-to-face conversation with Fey," I said.

Joe looked unsure and reluctant. The two women in his life were about to face off. It might get ugly.

"I have to talk to her." There was no room for negotiation.

Wearing a cream sleeveless silk top and a yellow mini-skirt, I examined myself in the mirror and approved how I looked. While my roommates were indulged in reading Chiung Yao's stories of complex and heart-melting love triangles, I was living it. I was about to fight for the love of my life!

I arrived at Fey's dorm in the hospital. She opened the door. The room was very simple but neat with only a bed, a desk, and two chairs. Fey was in a black and white blouse and knee-high skirt. We were about the same height except she was a little heavier, and her weight seemed to gravitate to her hips. She had large brown eyes, a not so attractive nose, and a distinctive mouth. She offered me a drink and sat across from me, staring blankly at the floor.

I started, "Thank you for taking the time to meet with me. I've wanted to meet you for a while."

All of a sudden she sprang back to life, "I know you're upset with me spending time with Joe. But where were you when his father was dying? I was there every day. He cried on my shoulder. I did everything I could to support and comfort him."

My confidence flew out of the window. All of a sudden, I felt small and insignificant. It took a few seconds to pull myself back together and get the conversation on the right track.

"I'm grateful for what you've done for him and his family. My father and I are not close. I didn't understand the impact of his father's illness on him. But we love each other very much, and we are in the middle of working things out. I need you to leave us alone."

"I deserve another chance too!"

"It's a bit too late for that."

"Why? Life is so unfair! Both you and I made mistakes. How come I don't get a chance to make it right with him?"

"Because he loves me. We will get married as soon as we can."

There was a long pause. "I know he loves you. I can tell. I should leave him alone … I'll leave you alone. You have my word." Unspoken anguish spread across her face.

"Thank you." I looked into her pretty brown eyes with a deep sense of empathy.

*Back then I had no doubt about my love for Joe. Today, without the danger of losing him to another woman and the power of God holding us together, do I still love him? Do I still love him the way I did thirty years ago?*

\*

*I was born at the start of Cultural Revolution*

*The teenager me*

*This picture was taken in Yun Nan with my father and sister*

*The teenager me in love*

*Married to Joe in 1988*

*Came to the U.S. in October of 1988*

一九八九年 五月 於 紐約 曼哈頓

*We lived in Manhattan when Joe pursued his Ph.D. in physics*

*Spent a few care free days sailing with David and Nancy*

102  *Let Go*

*With Jane and Grandma in Long Island, New York*

*Grandma and Jane*

*Michelle was born in 1995*

*With my precious girls*

*Jane and Michelle*

*Grandma surrounded by her grandchildren and great grandchildren. Grandma was terminally ill in this picture*

The building committee had a series of meetings in early 2008 to develop a new budget proposal. It looked like the construction would be close to $6.5M. Our previous budget didn't have a contingency fund, and so this time we raised it from zero to two hundred thousand dollars to give ourselves a little cushion.

Everyone on the committee felt too nervous and restricted to even suggest a budget bigger than $6.5M, although we knew the likelihood of going over was reasonably high. We hoped it wouldn't exceed $6.5m by over ten percent, which would make this the last congregational vote to approve a new budget.

Being a simple-minded person, I figured if I could convince myself that the increases were reasonable, I might have a chance of convincing the congregation that thought like me. Persuading the BOD would be a different story. Most of the board members had Ph.D. degrees and were highly technical. I was absolutely not looking forward to the budget discussion with them.

Ruth and I worked hard for the next couple of weeks. We made a list of all the items that contributed to the $1M budget jump and noted the reasons next to each item. What I came to understand through this exercise was that the quotes the contractors provided before construction started were often lower than what they were willing to sign on the dotted line of the contract. The constant design alterations cost us a bundle. We also left out some large sums of fees due to the government agencies.

The new budget caused an uproar in BOD. On top of Mr. Critic, Mr. Doubtful, Mr. Steward, and Mr. Righteous, I now had to deal with Mr. Angry, Mr. Concern, Mr. Process, and Mr. Justice. Ryan the Righteous said something that caught my attention.

"Evangelical Free Church completed their building extension project in nine months, and they didn't have to increase their budget once. Did any of you talk to them? If you don't know how to do it, why not just copy from someone who's done it before?" Ryan looked around the room, laughed eerily.

I fired back. "I've talked to one of their key building committee members. They started with a realistic budget and hired a professional construction firm to manage the project. In the end the pricy sound system was taken out to keep the construction under budget. Even though it looked easy from the outside, there were internal struggles that caused over ten percent of the congregation to leave the church."

*Wait a minute ... could Ryan be Mr. Copycat? Joe collaborated with him on a few business ideas but none ended up going anywhere. Is he capable of copying Joe's ideas and then claim they're his own?*

The board meeting was emotionally draining as expected, but once again I was given the green light to present the budget to the congregation on the Sunday of the following week.

Saturday night I was a nervous wreck, unsure how the church as a whole was going to take the bad news in double doses: schedule delay and cost surge. I would be pretty worried sitting on the receiving end of the bad news.

In my dream that night I was going to present the budget through the radio station in the junior high school building. The radio was on when I arrived, but I couldn't find the broadcast room. I climbed the stairs hurriedly and went to every floor and every room, and then the voice in the radio announced, "That's it for today. Goodbye!"

I collapsed and let out a scream, "But I haven't even got a chance to present the budget yet!"

Dressing appropriately for the occasion was always a good place to start. I put on an antique, ruby V-neck silk sweater and black suit trousers. The addition of a black stone Y necklace with matching earrings offered a touch of professionalism. I wanted to look formal but not stiff, serious but thoughtful, calm but not cold.

After setting my stuff down on one of the seats in the front row, I went to the bathroom to calm my nerves. I always had the urge to empty my bladder whenever feeling nervous. My presentation would be at the end of the service, after the music worship, the sermon, and the announcements. I wished I could do it right away to get over with.

The worship leader stepped onto the stage. The service was about to begin. I looked around, and as usual, the gym was packed. We had been having Sunday worship here for eight years. Every Sunday morning, whether rain or shine, stormy or snowy, a van would arrive outside the door carrying all the sound system equipment. Volunteers would set up and test the system.

Then hundreds of metal folding chairs would be lined up in front of the movable stage that basically was just a big wooden box. This church had started with thirty-five families. Now the size of the Mandarin congregation was well over three hundred. Right after the worship, the sound system would be taken apart, the chairs stacked up and pushed back to the storage area and long tables and benches pulled out from the walls to allow for lunch fellowship joined by the children, youth, and the English congregation. It was a lot of work, and many faithful brothers and sisters had made sacrifices week in and week out so we could gather here every week to worship God. We really needed our own church building!

"Now Church Building Deacon Linda Xu will present the new budget proposal and schedule projection." Scott announced at the end of the service.

I stood up, making sure I had all the notes in my hand and walked towards the stage. Once on stage, I slowly spread my notes on the podium and looked up at the audience. All eyes were on me, and I knew the question on everyone's mind "When is the new church going to be done?"

"The church building ministry has certainly been a long and difficult journey. We still have more obstacles to overcome before getting to the final destination. Today I am going to share with you the new budget proposal and a revised timeline."

I went through the numbers and the reasons in enough but not too much detail. To put things into perspective, I told the congregation a personal story. "Last fall, Joe and I decided to replace our old kitchen windows. We obtained quotes from a few contractors. It was not going to be cheap. So Joe looked up the Home Depot website and figured out how much the material would cost. He then contacted a window installer to get an estimate on the labor cost. Adding the two together, we would save about $7,000 if we purchase the windows on our own and have Mr. Wang do the installation. And that was exactly what he did. The windows arrived at the end of October. Mr. Wang showed up mid-November hoping to get the job done quickly. But Joe's measurement was off so slightly that the new windows wouldn't fit perfectly. Mr. Wang said this would require more work, and he would have to come back. Then snow and freeze started. Just like our church building had to wait until spring to have the roof put on, we had no choice but to leave the bulky new windows in the garage the whole winter and park one of our cars on the driveway. I had to remind myself throughout the winter when I had to get into a freezing car that we were doing this to save money.

"Our church is doing the same thing. In order to cut cost, we are doing a lot of the legwork on our own instead of outsourcing the whole project. We are the construction general manager. I understand it is taking longer than expected and I understand that we are not very good at projecting costs …" I had the urge to apologize but resisted. None of us had prior experience with building a big church and all of us on the building committee had been doing the best we could with what we had.

"From the research I have done, building a 43,000 square foot church with $6.5m is very reasonable. We have been careful with the money given to us and diligent in our bidding process. I just got my beautiful new kitchen windows installed after a long winter. In the same way, we will have a new building in the near future. So please hang in there with us, it has been a wild ride, to say the least. We will continue to count on your support, your prayer, and your generous donation."

With that, I concluded the most difficult presentation of my life. Silence followed, as if the audience was trying to decide how to react. I froze. Someone applauded, joined by a few more, and then the whole gym burst into thunderous applause. I wanted to cry, but instead I smiled.

Before I even had the chance to pat myself on the back for a job well done, another crisis arose which threatened to keep the construction from moving ahead. Ruth submitted her resignation a couple of weeks after the budget presentation citing personal health reasons. We hadn't paid her and Rick for six months due to the idle mode of the construction even though she had been working day and night in an effort to get it going again. Losing Ruth would be a heavy blow to the building ministry. I dreaded going to the April BOD meeting that occurred the first Saturday of every month.

The BOD meeting started with song worship, Bible verse sharing by a designated person and around-the-table praying by twenty or so board and staff members. We always prayed for unity.

Under the spirit of unity, we were expected to make constructive remarks or criticism that built each other up instead of tearing each other down. That was the intent.

After praying, it was time for departmental updates. When it came to my turn to give a report on the building ministry, I expressed sadness and distress over Ruth's resignation.

"Do you know the real reason why she quit?" Mr. Concern questioned.

"Well, for one thing, she hasn't been paid for six months. I know she does have some health problems." I scanned the faces around the table, quite certain that none of us would stick with our job if the company we worked for refused to pay us.

"Why haven't we paid her?" Mr. Justice was indignant.

"I have informed you about this before. Shawn feels that the construction hasn't made much progress since last fall and thus decided to withhold both Rick and Ruth's pay."

"What is the decision process within the building committee? How could Shawn make such important decisions by himself?" Mr. Process jumped in outraged.

"Ruth reports into Shawn who is the head of the building committee. I did raise my concern, but ultimately it was his call."

"Why haven't these issues been brought to BOD before?" Mr. Critic complained.

"I didn't think it would become a huge issue. And I did bring it up to you before. None of you thought it was a problem either, since Ruth herself said she would stay on the project with or without pay."

"The building committee is so disorganized and chaotic. No wonder our new building is still standing out there without a roof. BOD is not getting informed on everything we need to know. We'll have to step in and get more involved!" Mr. Process boomed.

Blood rushed to my head and everything said afterwards became blah, blah, blah. I was overwhelmed by a sensation I had felt before when things got unbearably stressful. A horrific memory floated to the surface:

*I was nine years old, rolling on the floor screaming and kicking, with my hands covering my head. My mother smacked me repeatedly and mercilessly with a wooden toy rifle. Suddenly the gun broke ...*

Gripped by an urge to run away from it all, I fled out of the BOD meeting room sobbing. Joe knew I was not looking forward to the BOD meeting. When I came home early in tears, he knew the meeting didn't go well.

"Tell me who bullied you, I'll go there and teach them a lesson." He held me and rubbed my back.

"They are accusing me of hiding things from them. We sent them meeting minutes and invited them repeatedly to join the building committee discussions to get involved. Of course nobody bothered to come. I provided them with progress updates every month. Seriously, if I had brought every issue to the BOD meeting, there would have been more arguments and bickering and nothing would have ever gotten done. I can't do this anymore. I am too tired." I wept in his arms.

"How about we take a break from Living Water?" Joe had wanted a break for a while. He was only there because I had to be there.

"Okay. Let me send Scott a resignation letter right now. Tomorrow we'll go to the Calvary Church for Sunday service. I've already checked them out online."

> *Please accept my apology for walking out of the meeting. I have been feeling inadequate and incapable of serving as the church building deacon for a while. This job has taken a toll on my family and me. Please accept my resignation from BOD.*

After typing the note, it was as if a heavy weight was lifted from my shoulder. I looked outside. It was a sunny and warm early spring day.

"'Do you want to take Jake to the park? It's such a nice day.'" I turned to Joe.

"Why not? Let's go!"

We were going to celebrate little Jacob's second birthday in a couple of days. He had been my de-stressor and main source of joy and laughter in the past two years. At the age of two, Jake already talked like a little man.

He would say to me, "Mommy, the way you just said that to me didn't sound nice. You need to say sorry."

"I am sorry, baby. I didn't mean to hurt your feelings. Will you forgive me?" I tried to hold back from laughing.

"Yes! I love you, Mommy!" He ran over to hug me.

"I love you more, baby!" I kissed his chubby cheeks, and he giggled.

Once in the park, Jake was busy running around trying different things. Joe and I sat on the bench watching him. He got on the seesaw.

"Daddy, come and play with me."

Joe walked over and sat on the other end of the beam. The balance was off.

I joined them and sat behind Jake. Now we got it going, up and down, up and down. Jake's happy laughter filled the air.

The joyous and fragrant spring breeze brought clarity and focus to my mind. I felt ashamed of the way I handled the situation. How could I lose my composure like that?

*I am not a quitter! I have Grandma's blood running in me. She never quit no matter how difficult things got. She had a responsibility to her family, and she fulfilled that responsibility till her last breath. Whenever Jane and Michelle came to me and asked for permission to quit piano or Chinese, my answer had always been, "We are not quitters. Learning is good for you and you'll have to continue on."*

*Why am I running away? Even though I don't expect anything tangible from serving God in the church, I do yearn for something intangible: validation, admiration, acceptance, and praise. But the church building experience has brought back painful childhood memories where I was often the focus of contention, I could never do anything right, I was stupid and ugly ...*

Then I thought about Ruth, Shawn, and Maryann, the key members of the building committee. We had a strong team with distinctive personalities that didn't always blend well. Ruth took a soft approach, while Maryann had no problem challenging Shawn head-to-head.

"Shawn, the timeline you put together looks good on paper. The only issue I have is that there are still so many unknowns, so we can't commit to the dates."

"I have to put down something as goals for us to work towards." Shawn got defensive.

"But then you start talking about these dates as if they were real. People get disappointed when we don't deliver. That's how we lose our credibility."

"What am I supposed to do, not say anything?"

"How about this, from now on, we'll let Linda be the single voice from the committee? That's her job anyway."

"I'll stop talking if you do as well."

I glanced at Shawn nervously. The usual broad smile on his face disappeared. He slumped in his seat, looking beat.

"Okay! I'll stop talking." Maryann concluded with an honest smile.

Over the last two years, I had become an integral part of this dysfunctional but incredibly motivated team. I admired their dedication, persistence, and hard-working spirit. Quitting would mean letting each of my team members down.

"I am done. I want to go home now," Jake declared.

Jake always told us what he wanted or didn't want in his childish straightforward manner. *How wonderful it could be if we adults were childlike as Jake!*

My absence from Living Water on Sunday was felt. Rev. Zhong came to our house after the service. I had already told Joe that it was neither appropriate nor professional to walk away the way I did.

"I'd better get my ass back there and get the job done," I said jokingly.

Joe laughed and said he would support me either way. Rev. Zhong was very happy to hear that. Now we had to figure out a way to get Ruth back. She was critical to the project.

A few days later, Ruth and Luke agreed to sit down with the two pastors of the church, Scott, Shawn, and me to talk. The atmosphere was tense with a hint of unpredictability in the air. I asked Shawn to please stay calm and be a good listener because our goal was to win Ruth back. He promised he would.

Luke made no effort to hide how he felt about Shawn. I got a hunch of why he quit from the building committee. Luke accused Shawn of treating his wife unfairly, while Shawn argued that he did everything for the sake of the church. A few times during the discussion, Luke was about to bolt out of the room while Shawn fought to stay put.

At one point Ruth turned to Shawn and asked him bluntly, "It just seemed that you were never happy with how I did my job. If there was anything I did wrong, could you just tell me what it was?"

"No, no, no. I know you worked very hard. You didn't do anything wrong. It's just, it's just that we have a tight budget, and it's taking much longer than expected," Shawn stuttered.

In the end, the two men symbolically shook hands, and Ruth was back on the job with significantly less pay. I knew all along that she didn't want to quit in the first place, and that she wasn't doing it for money.

Like boxers who get knocked down hard but manage to stand up before the end of the countdown, the team was back together, ready to continue the fight.

\*

The transformation I went through in Jesus Christ was nothing short of a miracle. When I was a child, I was frequently called Lin Daiyu, a character from the book *Dream of the Red Chamber*. Due to the death of her mother, she moved into Ronguo House, the home of her cousin, Jia Baoyu. There she was well taken care of physically but she always felt like an outsider. Daiyu was beautiful, talented but fragile and sorrowful. I was unhappy like her a lot of times as if I was craving for something unobtainable. I channeled my energy to school work and got a lot of satisfaction out of it. But it was not enough. When I met and fell in love with Joe, love and stability entered my life that was badly needed. I married right after college and came to the United States while Joe was pursuing his Ph.D. Our marriage went through plenty of ups and downs. He was stable and mature, but I wasn't. I was still looking for that unobtainable thing.

Loving me was not easy. I gave a lot but expected no less back. My mood swings were difficult to handle. I now believed that the women in my family suffered from chronic depression. On those long nights after the bitter confrontations with Yan, Grandma would stare blankly ahead, tears rolling down her cheeks, murmuring the same thing over and over again. "My life is worthless. Everything is worthless. I'd better just put a rope around my neck and end this misery." I would stay awake just to make sure she didn't do anything silly.

Out of the five children, my mother was the least favored by my grandparents. Grandma treasured Aunt due to the loss of the three boys. But getting another girl right after Aunt was a disappointment. According to Grandma, Mother was extremely willful and unwise and therefore received more than her fair share of corporal punishment. Shortly after she married my father, he was sent to Yun Nan to be reformed. Mother stayed in Shanghai for a while and then decided to join my father. Everyone advised her to pay a visit and check things out first. But her mind was made up. She wanted to be with her husband. After she got there, they were still forced to live apart because most of the time they were assigned to different projects and thus had to live on different sites.

When the Cultural Revolution started, a bad situation got even worse for my parents. In my father's case, he was denounced at every public meeting in which he was forced to bow his head and wear a big sign in front of his chest that said "I am a descent of a capitalist. I deserve to die." My parents fled to Shanghai when I was a little over one to escape the life-threatening violence fanned by the national police chief's declaration that it was 'no big deal' if Red Guards were beating 'bad people' to death. As a result different groups all claiming to defend Maoism were fighting against and killing each other and many innocent 'bad people.'

My parents were so traumatized that they burned all their money on the balcony of 930 Long and threw away their jewelries in the Huangpu River. Because the more possessions the Red Guards could find and confiscate in the targets' home, the more guilty they became.

Father managed to escape more brutal punishment because he was never caught saying anything politically incorrect in public.

For over a decade, he was passed for any promotion or salary increase. Father never expected anything. He just wanted to be left alone. To numb himself, he turned to alcohol and cigarettes for relief.

My father's heavy drinking and smoking caught up with him eventually. His eczema and bronchitis condition worsened and stopped him from living a normal life at the end of the Cultural Revolution in 1976 when things were finally looking up for him, an accountant with a college degree and many years of experience.

Being the wife of a man who was the target of the Revolution which put my parents under constant scrutiny, humiliation, and persecution, the forced separation and responsibility to take care of my sick father most of her married life turned my mother to a bitter, explosive, and fearful human being. Mother would become violent when she couldn't contain her anger. Smacking me in Yun Nan was not the last time she ever hit me. She did it every time when she came back to Shanghai, which fortunately was only once every four years. One time, Yiwen took some money from her purse. She started yelling and screaming at her when she found out. Then she picked up the brown and black wooden toy rifle the size of a real one and turned to me. Her hair stood up, her face distorted, her pupils dilated. She desperately needed an outlet to dump the boiling rage inside her. The look on her face told me I would be her dumping ground, and so I dashed for the door but she grabbed me, pushed me to the floor and began spanking me with the rifle. For a small woman not even five feet tall, she had some strength. Every strike that landed on my butt or back hurt like hell. I screamed so loud that the whole neighborhood could hear it. The rifle broke. She finally stopped and walked out of the house. A few hours later Mother came back with a new perm and a smile on her face. She was a monster, not my mother. On the day she had to go back to Yun Nan, I purposely went home very late so that I didn't have to say goodbye to her.

Even though Aunt was a more lively and positive person, years of being squeezed between her mother and husband smothered her. She had the same blank stare as Grandma's when she cried, and I remembered she cried a lot. More than once she threatened to divorce Yan, but they always got back together. But her resentment was visible. Nowadays she just sat in a chair unresponsive to anything happening around her.

None of the women sought treatment. They didn't even know depression was a mental illness. And they kept on going as if it were just a headache that would eventually go away. Sometimes it did.

I had what I used to call the winter blues that sometimes spilled over to spring and summer, or pre-started in fall. Just feeling low didn't articulate why I was unhappy. Like Grandma, I kept myself doing what I was supposed to do even though something inside was dragging me down. Every once in a while, I would explode and make life temporarily unbearable for those around me, especially Joe.

My postpartum depression after giving birth to Jane and Michelle was pretty awful. I would cry for no reason and at times felt really trapped. My mother-in-law came to the United States after Michelle was born to help us out. She had been living in a two-story house in Pudong all by herself, the same house Gjyn and Mitch spent the weekend. So she cleaned up her house and gave one set of the keys to her neighbor asking them to keep an eye on the house since she would be gone for a while. My mother-in-law was seventy-five years old. She dyed her white hair black, combed it all back and bobby-pinned the sides behind her ears. Her footsteps were loud and swift and her ways of doing things were pretty set. She always went to the bathroom without turning on the lights or locking the door. I would jump when I opened the door and realized she was in there. She tried to use the minimum amount of water to wash anything, so all the dishes and cups were greasy. Her red cooked pork looked like charcoal and tasted awful. And above all she loved to tell people what to do. After about a month, I had it up to my eyeballs with her. I began to complain non-stop to Joe about his mother whom I began to view as an invasion of my home. Joe was stuck between two women he loved the most, not a good place to be.

I just gave birth and my hormones were doing a bungee jump. One day I pushed back when she was being bossy, and she started wiping tears with her handkerchief. Joe got so mad that he yelled at me for the first time since I had known him. I yelled back, "If you love your mother so much, why don't you live with her from now on?"

I put baby Michelle in the car and drove away trembling with fear and excitement. The problem was I never knew where I was going. I had no sense of direction, another wonderful inheritance from my mother. We just moved to Chicago, and I had no friends. After driving a few miles, I turned around and went home.

When the storm passed and both of us calmed down, Joe, being mature one, apologized. "I am sorry for yelling at you. But she is my mother. How could you treat her like that?"

"I am sorry, too. Our home has become so unpleasant and tense that I couldn't take it anymore. I just snapped," I sobbed.

"Maybe I should take her with me when I go to China in a couple of weeks for my conference. There is no way I am going to leave you two here alone."

"Is she going to be mad? She has told everyone that she'd be here for a while."

"She is my mother. She loves me. I'll take care of it. It'll work out," Joe assured me.

The wound this rift caused lasted longer than his mother's short stay. We also held conflicting views on parenting. He came from a family of eight kids and had a much more relaxed parenting style. Joe believed that kids should be encouraged to do things on their own at a very young age. Grandma did everything for me. She spoon fed me until I was five or six, braided my hair every day, even piggybacked me to the elementary school. So I did everything for Jane and Michelle. Plus it would be faster that way since I was always in a time crunch. I kept Jane and Michelle very busy by taking them to ballet lessons, skating practice, Chinese School, piano lessons, and tennis classes. Joe thought it was a waste of time and money, as kids should have a lot of down time to explore and figure out their own interests. We were also at odds with each other with regards to material stuff. I enjoyed buying them toys and other things, and Joe blamed me for spoiling them. In my mind, he was a stingy fun-spoiler.

We were a loving couple most of the time. But when the girls acted up, he would criticize the way I was raising them. We would end up arguing followed by a cold war. I longed for a more harmonious and intimate relationship. Neither of us knew how to get there. If I raised any concerns, he would just say, "Things are just fine. Why are you always complaining?"

One weekend I attended a marriage workshop at church. It struck me that I had been rebellious and disobedient in my relationship with Joe and with God. God made husband the head of the family and wife the helper. I had been trying to be the head all along. I was tearing my family down with my own hands. After much praying and reflection, I left a letter under Joe's pillow on Valentine's Day.

*Dear Joe, my love,*

*I have offended you and God in the past years by being controlling and not allowing you to fulfill your role as the leader of the family. Please forgive me.*

*From this day on, with God's grace, I will try to love you, obey you and help you.*

*Love, Your wife*

Joe was touched by my honesty and sincerity. He hugged me with, "I love you too, baby!" But his eyes said something different: "How long is this fever going to last?" Joe soon came to the pleasant realization that this fever was going to stay. Slowly but surely I started to change. Instead of forcing my ways, I prayerfully reminded myself to listen and comprise. If Joe felt strongly about something after we discussed it, I followed his lead.

Joe was the one who wanted to move into a newer, nicer house instead of spending a fortune fixing our old house. I went house hunting with him for a few weeks. It was like he had something in mind, and no house we saw matched the picture in his head. So I gave up, and he continued the search. Finally he found a house that met his criteria of quality, comfort, and affordability. We made an offer. The housing market was hot in 2001. Within hours, we were told another contract had just been submitted with a higher offer price. Our realtor was anxious to close the deal.

"Add another $5,000 and the house may very likely be yours."

Joe cleared his throat. "If they like it that much, they can have it. I am not going to start a price war."

*$5,000 is nothing when we are buying a house close to half a million dollars. Why don't we just up the price and get it over with? I like the house. It has a walkout basement to a lovely pond*, I thought to myself. I looked at Joe. He wasn't going to budge. So I kept my mouth shut.

Of course we didn't get the house. Joe told me later that he would raise the offer price if he absolutely loved the house. But he didn't. He just liked it. Joe lost his job later that year, so it was a good thing that we didn't have a bigger mortgage. *Wow, God really knows everything. We are in safe hands if we just obey him.*

In the hospital when Dr. Simon advised us not to fly to China, I had no intention of listening to him. But when Joe finally decided to cancel our trip, I realized it was from God. This was the result of years of praying, reflection, and obedience. And that saved my life! I was convinced that one way to show my obedience to God was to obey the man whom he had chosen to be my husband.

My winter blue became more infrequent and shorter lived. Every time I sensed that I was heading in the wrong direction, I prayed this prayer to God: "Dear God, I don't want to go to that dark and lonely place again. Help me turn around and lift up my spirit. I want to live a joyful life that is pleasing to you." With that awareness, most of the time, I was able to change course before depression got the better of me.

"How am I doing as your darling, obedient wife?" I followed the teaching from the workshop to seek feedback from time to time.

"Your heart is all there, but there is resistance in your bones." Joe often gave me the same answer with a wink.

Joe was telling the truth. When he insisted that I held on to the Sears stock and within two weeks its value decreased by fifty percent, it took every ounce of power in my body not to say, "I told you so." But my body language gave away what my tongue held back.

In spite of the resistance in my bones, Joe developed a deep appreciation and adoration for me as I went through the transformation. The wall between us fell down and we were able to enjoy an intimate, trusting relationship that was out of this world.

To me, Christian faith wasn't dessert. It was dinner, essential to my daily living and wellbeing.

*

Joe's views towards God and religion continued to evolve. He now firmly believed evolution was undisputable. It was not only supported by traditional biology, but also by other academic disciplines such as anthropology, psychology, geology, and cosmology.

My concern continued to grow. I invited Lin and her husband Pastor Grant who held a Ph.D. in computer science to come to our home and chat with Joe. The friendly discussion soon turned into an emotional debate, with Joe dominating the conversation.

"Evolution theory is not set in the stone as you stated it. What about the missing links that haven't been found?" Pastor Grant challenged.

"There are no missing links. Now we possess a long and completed list of human evolution fossils." Joe spoke with an authoritative tone.

"That's not possible. Otherwise evolution would have been treated as science instead of a shaky theory."

"It is solid science. Outside the church walls, evolution has been accepted as proven science and has wide applications."

Before giving anyone a chance for rebuttal, Joe pushed on, "Even the Vatican no longer openly objects to the scientific evidence of evolution."

"But who started the whole process in the very beginning?" Grant asked.

"Quantum fluctuations. In quantum mechanics, matters are created from nothing and annihilated to nothing. This has been observed and tested. Our universe along with time and space can be created through quantum fluctuations. As a matter of fact, the cosmic microwave background radiation experiments show that the universe is flat and that in itself is an indication that the total energy-mass of the universe is zero…" Joe charged on with so much energy and conviction, totally oblivious to the fact that none of us had a clue of what he was talking about.

"Do you know that at the beginning of the big bang things moved faster than light? All the physics laws didn't apply at that point of time. Who defined the law of nature? Science can't explain. It can't even explain where time comes from. It's God who created and defined everything for us." Grant wasn't going to back down either. Apparently, he had done his homework for this discussion.

"We know things moved faster than light at the beginning. Even as we speak, things at the edge of our universe are moving faster than the speed of light. That's because the universe is expanding faster than the speed of light, and it can be explained within the realm of physics law. The time and space of the universe…"

"Joe, I haven't read as much as you have," Lin piped up before Joe had a chance to finish his elaborated lecture. "Even if evolution is true, it still doesn't bother me because I know God is real. And I'll continue to believe in Him," Lin stated her position without any ambiguity.

"I respect that. I was able to ignore the facts of evolution before my brother passed away. But now I can't."

"We can understand that," Grant responded empathetically.

Joe's tone softened, "If God is real, the seventy or eighty years we live on the earth are so insignificant compared to the eternal life he offers us. If God is real, I should quit my job as a scientist, go to seminary like you did, and serve God full time. I was actually at the turning point of my life," Joe paused for second, then added, "but after all the research, I've come to the conclusion that the God described in the Bible isn't real. There is no eternal life. We simply disappear after death."

The air in the room went stiff. I noticed the sadness and anguish in Lin and Grant's eyes. I put my head down.

Joe went on, "I also spent considerable amount of time studying the human brain. The need for God is genetically coded in our brain as a result of evolution. That explains why in the face of all the scientific evidence, people still choose to ignore the facts and continue to cling onto God…"

"Joe, you are obviously very intelligent. Grant and I pray that someday, you will turn back to God. You are his child. He will never give up on you." Lin sounded disheartened and yet hopeful and certain.

Most people argued that science was so limited that it couldn't explain everything, especially God. I found it interesting that the same people didn't find science limiting when it came to medicine, dieting, or child education, and yet when it challenged the authority of the Bible, science had to be wrong or unreliable. Joe explained to me that science is a methodology that studies the natural world by forming and testing hypotheses, constructing scientific theories, using observational data, and performing experiments in both the field and the laboratory. It is the most objective tool that has helped the human race advance its knowledge of themselves and the world they live in. I agreed with him on that part.

The Christian scientists who debated Joe had no trouble accusing other scientists of being too egotistical as they dared to claim having answers to things that only God could possibly have answers to. I had witnessed this firsthand in the BOD meeting room and seriously doubted how many so-called Christians truly possessed Christ-like humbleness. In fact, outsiders often viewed Christians as more arrogant because there was a deep-rooted conviction that they were better than the others as God's chosen ones. They were going to heaven, and the rest would end up in hell.

Joe's confrontational debate style was bothersome. I was afraid his insensitivity and forcefulness might drive some of our long-time friends away. On the other hand, there was still a little girl in me who admired that handsome young man, a graduate student from Shanghai Jiao Tong University, and wanted to believe he knew everything. His training as a physicist required him to gather data, analyze, and draw conclusions based on facts. I'd like to believe he wouldn't say something he knew was totally untrue just to offend our friends. But the strong reaction from others made me realize facts to some might be nonsense to others. Most people couldn't be bothered to check things out, me included. Faith was such a personal thing facts really didn't matter as much.

In my church, we were taught that evolution was one of the many theories explaining how life came into being, and it was false. God created us humans with his spirit, glory, and dignity, and therefore we simply couldn't be descendants of monkeys. A couple of Christian biologists who came to our church preached that microevolution was true, but not macroevolution. This had become most people's default view towards evolution.

Joe was often questioned about his view on miracles. He would flatly say that all miracles we had witnessed had a statistical chance of happening no matter how small that chance was. If a person with stage IV lung cancer found out his cancer had disappeared, to him it would undoubtedly be a miracle. But this could happen to a very small percent of the cancer patients who would be cured with or without any treatment. On the other hand, it would be statistically impossible for a person who lost an arm or leg to grow a new one. And that explained why it hadn't happened in the medical history.

His assertion that soul didn't exist was even more over the top. To him, if soul existed, it should have interacted with the other parts of the body or the outside world. Since no scientific evidence could be found to prove such interaction, it didn't exist.

"If our brain is just a whole bunch of hardware connected together with no software, we are totally pathetic! Joe, I can't believe you have descended as low as this!" Our friend Jean protested indignantly. She and her husband, Hahn, had moved to a different state and stayed with us for a weekend during one of their visits.

Jean called me after they got back home, genuinely concerned about Joe's current radical views. "I have no idea he has been in such a dark place ... he must be really depressed and lost."

"He isn't depressed as far as I know." I assured her.

"I'm concerned about you too. How are you holding on? Has he changed his ways towards you?"

Jean was the first one who verbalized a concern for me with the change in Joe's religious views. "I'm doing OK. I was brought on this crazy ride not out of my own choice, but I am on it. We'll figure this out."

The next time we talked Jean repeated her conviction that Joe was in a state of depression and was worried about my wellbeing.

"Jean, if you're feeling sorry for us, please don't. This is part of the life experience. We'll figure it out. I don't need anyone to feel sorry for me, really!"

Jean's husband Hahn was a full professor of computer science in a prominent university. He hadn't aged at all in the last fifteen years, still slow to voice his opinion and walking around with a black backpack. If you ran into him on campus, you would have thought he was one of the students instead of an accomplished professor. Hahn decided to look into Joe's arguments and prove they were wrong. Hahn conducted some extensive probability calculation and traded emails back and forth with Joe. "Joe, according to my calculation, the probability of human coming from evolution is one out of 10 to the $46000000^{th}$. The number of atoms in the entire observable universe is estimated to be within the range of 10 to the $78^{th}$ to $82^{nd}$. Therefore, it is simply not possible that humans are evolved. They have to be created."

Joe wrote back, "I have no doubt your numbers are correct. However, your assumptions are completely wrong. You are mixing the after-the-fact result with the before-the-fact probability. If you look at a rock in your backyard, the probability of all the atoms and molecules being arranged in this particular way is way smaller than the probability you calculated for human evolution. Therefore, according to your calculation, it should not be there. Yet it is.

"When Einstein came up with the general relativity theory based on scientific observations and claimed that space actually could be bent by gravity, the scientific community had a very heated debate. But the general public simply accepted his claim after the debate cooled down. Darwin's theory that humans are evolved from earlier apes based on scientific observations has been supported by one hundred and fifty years of scientific findings and facts, but the general public just can't accept it, simply because of the religious beliefs…"

I didn't know who was right or what to believe anymore. Seeing my torment, Joe offered a solution, "If it makes you happy, I'll believe in God again … I can try."

I was moved by his warm gesture. As badly as I wanted things to go back to the way they were, I couldn't ask him to do that. After all, he was the one who lost his father, sister, and brother to cancer. If that didn't make him pause and ask questions, there would have been something wrong with him. Plus forcing him to believe for my sake would be comparable to making him stay after he had fallen in love with another woman. It would be meaningless and joyless. *Still, there is no other way but to continue on with the ride and see where it takes us.*

*

The online war between Joe and Mr. Copycat intensified and turned into a price war. Things were sold almost at cost. One day Joe received an anonymous threat through our company website claiming we were not a legitimate business, and they would notify others via Internet newsgroups.

Joe started conducting more business offline by working with established distributors. Since our brand name was well recognized online, distributors were more than willing to work with us.

Our home phone was also ringing more frequently especially in the middle of the night. Men would call and ask for Jessica. I usually told them they had the wrong number and hung up. It got disturbing when Jane and Michelle complained about guys calling late at night and speaking to them in sexually explicit words. I asked one of the callers where he got my number and realized our phone number had been listed on multiple porn sites along with a picture of a half-naked "Jessica." We called the Naperville police department. Detective Johnson took the case.

*Our phone number is listed in the church directory, could this person be someone we know ... from church? Could it be Mr. Copycat? Could he be so low as to do something like this?*

Meanwhile the road to the new building continued to be bumpy and winding. The $6.5M budget was exceeded within a few months. Now it was heading towards $6.8M. Fortunately with all things considered, it looked like another congregational vote wouldn't be necessary since we wouldn't go over the ten percent threshold.

Ruth hired a few temporary handymen to handle some of the small jobs on site. Jorge was one of them. One day a piece of construction material fell and hit Jorge on the shoulder. He was injured. Jorge didn't have a full time job at the time and thus no medical insurance.

The next morning, I got a call from Keri, a very active and influential church volunteer who had made significant contributions to the new building ministry. I had a lot of respect for her.

"Linda, have you heard about the accident yesterday?" Keri asked cautiously.

"Yes, I have. We need to figure out a way to handle the situation quickly."

"Since most of the contractors are self-insured, our church only bought insurance for the building. I am worried how much this is going to cost us. I want to tell you that I've asked the administration deacon to remove Ruth's picture from the church's website."

"Why did you do that?" I was astounded.

"Well, when we hired Ruth as the project manager, we didn't sign a contract with her. At her request, we signed a contract with the company under her husband's name."

"I know that. She did that for accounting purposes. But what's that got to do with removing her picture?"

"You see, Living Water didn't hire Jorge, Luke's company did. So in that sense we aren't liable for the accident." The subtleness in her voice was replaced by a sense of relief.

I was dumbfounded. *Ruth didn't hire Jorge to do work for her house. She hired him exclusively for the new building. Who gave Keri the right to instruct the administration deacon to remove Ruth's picture anyway? Where is Mr. Process when we needed him?* In the spirit of unity and because of my tendency to avoid confrontations especially with people I like, I held back what was already on the tip of my tongue. Instead, "I am sure BOD will do the right thing for everyone involved."

"Yes, I know. I just want to give you the heads up."

"Okay, thanks." I hung up the phone.

The phone call, as disturbing as it was, made one thing clear. The church was an institution. In the face of crisis, some would do whatever it took to protect its own interest. This might explain why the Catholic sex abuse cases had caused so much outrage, not just because of the abuse itself but also because of the lengthy cover-up and inaction. Living Water might be insignificant compared to the Vatican, but the desire to protect was nevertheless the same. I made a decision that day: I was going to leave this institution once the new building was finished.

Scott, the BOD chair, took charge of handling the Jorge incident. Living Water ended up hiring a lawyer and made a payout to Jorge.

Call it a miracle or whatever; the building finally came together two years after construction started. The pressure to get it done was mounting. We were throwing money at the contractors to buy speed. The final construction cost reached $7M.

In October, I organized the move-in cleanup. The majority of the congregation showed up, young and old, male and female, healthy and weak. Everyone pulled up his or her sleeves and got to work. The big, dusty building was bustling with activity, mopping, vacuuming, dusting, wiping, and scrubbing. There was a song in the air! Like the Israelites who finally entered the promise land after wandering in the dessert for forty years, we, the Asian Christian community in Naperville, were coming home. It was a bittersweet day for me. I was proud of what we had accomplished as a community but sad knowing I wouldn't stay at this home much longer.

The new building dedication ceremony was held early November, three years after the groundbreaking ceremony. With the help of Ruth, Shawn, Maryann, and Pastor Grant, I put together a slide presentation depicting the construction process and the involvement of the whole congregation. Mayor Pradel called it heartwarming and again welcomed Living Water to the City of Naperville.

Joe, Jake, and I left Living Water, our spiritual home, in December of 2009.

*

"Welcome to the Compass Church!" A man with a broad smile held the door with his back and extended his hand to us as we walked into the church building. His face and nose had turned red from standing out in the cold. But his smile was heartwarming. I shook his hand. "Thank you!"

The Compass Church was the former Evangelical Free Church. We used to have our Friday Bible study fellowship in their basement classrooms. They had expanded their old church building by adding a modern theater-style auditorium.

There are two morning worship services on Sunday. The earlier session had just ended. People were standing in the atrium hugging, talking, and laughing. It was weird but at the same time relieving to be in a church surrounded by all these nice-looking people, and yet I had no connection with any of them. We zigzagged through the crowd to get Jake checked in at Sunday school. Jake needed a little encouragement to enter the classroom, and then he headed straight to the toys on the floor.

Joe and I made our way to the balcony. The music worship had already started. The auditorium had the seating capacity of one thousand. I knew because I had talked to one of the elders in charge of the church expansion project. This building was clearly of higher quality than ours. The concrete floor was smooth and without cracks, the lighting soothing and inviting, the million dollar sound system definitely worth every penny, and the colorful stage lights added liveliness and focus to the action on the stage. The Compass Church frequently hosted Christian concerts in this beautiful sanctuary.

Surrounded by lively music, joyful singing from the worship team, and an enthused congregation, I wondered what internal conflicts could have caused all those people to leave this beautiful church during the expansion. I decided I didn't want to know. I felt completely out of place and homesick. I wanted to go back to my own church, as imperfect as it was, because it had been my home, and I had helped build it. I glanced at Joe. He was enjoying himself, tapping his foot on the floor to the rhythm of the music, swaying back and forth. Joe was finally home! He had been feeling awkward and uncomfortable at Living Water for a couple of years. The preaching there didn't interest him anymore, and he wasn't sure what to do when the bread and cup were served for the Holy Communion. Not taking them would certainly raise eyebrows because everyone knew him as a Christian. So he started hanging out with Jake in his classroom. When Jake turned three, the teachers asked all the parents to leave in order to help the kids overcome separation anxiety. He wandered into one of the classrooms where parents with infants stayed. The sermon could be heard through a speaker, but he usually just sat behind the teacher's desk and read books.

I shifted my eyes to the energy-filled worship team of three on stage. They were bouncing to the rhythm of the music with eyes closed from time to time and fingers pointing to the sky whenever the name of God was shouted out. Their voices blended wonderfully together. The three big screens behind them projected vivid and color-rich pictures as well as the soul-touching lyrics. I allowed myself to indulge in the moment a little bit more.

Joe and I both found Pastor Dale's sermon refreshing. He knew his audience well and was able to connect with and speak to their hearts. Dale was in his fifties, of medium-built, and completely bald. He appeared sharp and easy to approach. He wasn't shy of making fun of his baldness. A skillful and experienced speaker, Dale preached eloquently, precisely, and passionately. He paused at the right time, for the right amount of time, and his gestures perfected how he delivered the message.

The sermon was short and to the point. The whole service was well planned and productionized. Very impressive! Above all, I could just sit there and enjoy the show without worrying about a thing! Jake liked attending Sunday school at Compass much more than at Living Water. It looked like we were here to stay.

*

Leaving Living Water was harder than I ever thought it would be. What I left behind was far more than a mere building. It was a whole world! A mourning process took place to mourn the losses of a close relationship with God, a community that supported and nourished me, friends I connected with every week, and an environment where my gifts and talents were put to good use. There was a void in my life: no new projects to tackle or challenges to conquer. I looked to Joe to fill that void but he quickly ran out of the tools in his toolbox. The sparkle in his eyes disappeared. He no longer did that awkward dance in front of me when we ran into each other in the house. Once again, we didn't know how to tear down the walls between us.

I was able to laugh and keep going everyday because of Jake. After dinner, Joe would bathe him, and then Jake and I would go upstairs to his room, reading books, playing, and cuddling. He would dump all his diapers on the floor and transport them to the garbage basket in his bathroom. Our little Jacob aspired to be a garbage collector when he grew up. I was amazed at how he never got bored doing the same thing over and over again. We always ended the night by Jake lying on my chest on the rocking chair. I slowly counted to one hundred while stroking his back with my fingers. He would put my hand back on his back to suggest more caressing. Jacob brought meaning to my life as I struggled to find purpose and new direction.

Ever since doubt crept into my mind about God, my relationship with him had changed from an intimate to a distant one. When I read the Bible, instead of hearing God speaking to me directly, the words ran into each other and didn't make much sense anymore. Whenever I prayed to God, seeking guidance and direction, I was more lost than ever. He probably was still talking to me, but the antenna on my end no longer pointed in the right direction to receive his messages. What disappointed me the most was that I was reverting back to the way I was before I became a born-again Christian. The transformation was being undone.

The old me was sad, broken, and self-centered. My winter blues came back full force. Many days I sat in front of the computer at work with teary eyes and a knot in my throat. When a colleague who was assigned to be my backup of a new process got aggressive about learning and taking over, I told her to shove it. "Calm yourself down. I'll teach you after I figure out how to do this myself." In the past, whenever I had Jane or Michelle in my car, I viewed it as a precious opportunity to communicate and connect with them. Now I grew quiet and withdrawn. I was on a lonesome journey with no light at the end of the tunnel.

Joe spent more time in front of the computer. He and I took Jake to the zoo, the Children's Museum, and the Children's Garden, but we had given up on sharing our innermost feelings and thoughts. I had got fed up listening to him going on and on about evolution, brain plasticity, and what death was about. Every time he and I did try to communicate, it somehow always ended up going back to same topics. So we stopped.

Joe still smiled and fell asleep easily at night. Sometimes I wished he would be capable of showing a wider range of emotions instead of being so together all the time. But I didn't know if I could handle it if he were not as stable and rational as he had always been.

I was again having trouble sleeping, an old problem I thought had been cured by God's healing power. Many nights I tossed and turned in bed feeling desperately lonely and exhausted, and sometimes I went from room to room trying to fall asleep. What Joe and I had shared in the past ten years could be more than what others had for a lifetime. I should be happy and content. But I wasn't. I wanted more. I knew there could be more.

*What do I really want in life? I crave love, family, validation, and acceptance. God gave me all of that, the church provided a platform to share my new life with the body of Christ, and Joe's love was as close to God's unconditional love as I could get from this world. But now the supply from God has stopped, I have separated from the church, and Joe and I are having problems relating to each other, where do I go from here? How long can I live like this without getting completely burned out?*

A pair of large innocent brown eyes stared at me in the darkness and penetrated my soul, her childish face full of agony and anticipation. I panted.

*What did that little girl want who was trapped in her aunt's home on those dreadful nights when her grandma was crying her eyes out and threatening to take her own life? She was all by herself, no God, no church, no Joe. What was she longing for?*

"What is it that you want?" I whispered to her.
"A home I can call my own."
"You have a home now with three beautiful kids and a husband. Your dream has come true!"
"But you are trying to destroy it, and you are miserable while doing it." A tear rolled down her cheek.

*She is right. I've got what I have always wanted in life and more. But can two self-centered people really make their love last a lifetime and build a loving home for their children without the presence of the supernatural power serving as the lubricant and glue?*

Even with a six-year-long courtship and a remarkable love story, we couldn't get our relationship to work until Joe and I invited Jesus to the top of our marriage triangle. Why would it work this time? How long and how much effort would it take? Could I even wait till that day?

\*

As soon as I fell in love with Joe, I couldn't stop dreaming of marrying him and building a family with him someday. He left for the United States during my senior year in college and the thought of being separated from him was devastating. He would be thousands of miles away, and even though we had promised to wait for each other, distance could change a lot of things. We wrote to each other constantly, and the mailman became my best friend those days.

A couple of months after he was gone, my class went on a weeklong internship trip to Wuxi to serve as translators for Western tour groups. I met David and Nancy from Canada on a tourist cruise ship. David was a successful Jewish businessman in his early sixties and Nancy, his wife, a homemaker. David was handsome, assertive, and talkative with a broad smile and a big belly. Nancy was petite and elegant. They made a great couple together. David and I were soon engaged in a deep conversation. I told him I was going to join my fiancé in New York after college.

"My business takes me to New York all the time. I'll go and visit you guys." He sounded like an old friend already. "What is he studying in New York?"

"He is pursuing a Ph.D. in physics."

"He must be really smart."

"Yes, he is!" I replied proudly, gazing into the glistening water. It was early November, and the wind was getting brisk and chilly.

"I bet you miss him a great deal."

"I sure do." I looked further ahead.

"Tell you what," he took out a mini tape recorder from his pocket, "record whatever you want to say to him. I'll mail the tape to him once I get back to Canada." He handed me the recorder with a fatherly smile on his face.

I got inside, sat down, turned the machine on, and started talking. Growing up I watched Yueju Opera with Grandma and learned how to sing it. So I sang to the recorder because Joe liked it. I totally forgot my role as the translator and poured my heart into this silvery device I held in my hand. When I finally pushed the stop button and looked up, the tourists were looking at me with tears in their eyes. They saw a young girl in love, which reminded them of their own young love.

Our chaplain, Mr. Shen, who took us to Wuxi decided he needed to go home and get some warm clothes. Some of my classmates asked him to bring them extra clothes as well. Mr. Shen left the whole class under my supervision and said he would be back in a couple of days. We stayed on a college campus in Wuxi. At dinnertime, the student cafeteria was packed and there were long lines in front of each serving window. I was standing in line with a few of my friends when a young guy approached us. He looked different from everyone else in the cafeteria: blue eyes, blond hair, not even tall by the Chinese standard but muscular.

"Where are you from?" he asked us with a charming grin.

"Oh, hi! We're from Shanghai. We are here on internships, translating for the tourists," one of my friends replied.

"And you?" I asked.

"I'm from New Zealand. I am here learning Chinese Kung Fu."

"Interesting! How do you like living here?" another girl chimed in.

"I like China, but I don't like this campus. The vegetables served here are so dead. They are always running out of hot water, and the power goes out a lot."

"Things must be very different in New Zealand. Are you homesick?" My giggly roommate was empathetic.

"It's OK. I am only going to be here for six months. They do make special dishes for me. I need to go to the kitchen. See you around!"

We sent him on his way in chorus, "Bye!"

I ran into Eric from New Zealand a few times, and we had small talks. He complained that there was no freedom in China. In New Zealand, he could get on TV anytime to say whatever was on his mind. The way he said it made me want to go to America even more.

A couple of days later he invited me to his room to show me some pictures of New Zealand. I went after dinner. Eric was obviously a good photographer with an impressive collection of beautiful scenery pictures. As I was flipping through the albums, the lights went out. He was prepared for the situation and quickly lit a couple of candles. The atmosphere changed. In the dim flickering light, his intense gaze made me really uncomfortable.

"Do you know how beautiful you are?" he sounded awfully gentle and sweet.

"Don't … I am here to look at your pictures … I am not interested in romance."

He stood up, came by my side, held me from the back and started kissing me on the neck. I was vulnerable. I missed my Joe. Eric slowly pulled me up from the chair I was sitting on, pushed me against the wall, pressed himself on me, and kissed me fervently. For a minute, I imagined I was back in Joe's arms. I lifted my head and met his kiss with my lips. When I opened my eyes, in the moonlight, two blue eyes were so close to my face that they made me want to jump.

*This is all wrong. I can't do this. I'll have to make him stop.*

I pushed Eric away. "Let go of me. We can't do this!"

"Why not?" He took a few steps back, panting heavily, and looking totally bewildered.

"Because it's against the teaching of the Bible!" I headed towards the door.

"You got to be kidding," he moaned.

I turned around and looked at him in the eye, "No, I'm not." I walked out and closed the door behind me.

Eric and I ran into each other again the next day, the day before we were heading back to Shanghai.

"I'm sorry for what happened last night. I was just, you know," he mumbled awkwardly.

"It's OK, no harm done." I looked away from his gaze.

"Could you stop by and say goodbye before leaving tomorrow morning?" He was almost begging.

*There is no way I am going back to his room again.*

"I promise I won't do anything. Just want to say goodbye."

*He isn't dangerous or violent. He's just lonely living in a foreign country by himself.*

"Alright. I'll stop by tomorrow morning."
"Great! See you then!"

I went to his room again super early in the morning before we had to get on the bus. We hugged and said goodbye. That was the last time I ever saw Eric from New Zealand.

David kept his promise and mailed the tape to Joe. Joe was thrilled to hear my voice and singing. David visited us shortly after I arrived in New York. He came to my office where I worked as a bankruptcy counselor and took me out to lunch. I was hired as a receptionist by Budget and Credit Counseling Services and was promoted to be a bankruptcy counselor within a month. I had no knowledge of credit and no credit cards of my own, but I was willing to learn and work hard. My boss saw that and told me that I was too smart to just be answering the phone. David also treated Joe and me to a fancy restaurant where we were pampered and served juicy and delicious lobsters. I loved David and Nancy like my own parents, and they treated me like their own daughter.

The first summer I was in New York, David and Nancy invited us to sail with them on their new boat, *Time Out*. David flew us to Vermont where the boat was anchored. It was a forty-one-foot sailboat with two cabins. We spent a few carefree days sailing and then drove to Canada and stayed in their apartment for a couple more days. They had quite a collection of souvenirs from all over the world. David was going to retire by the end of the year to sail around the world.

A week after we flew back to New York, I got a call from Nancy. "Hongwei, dear, I have very bad news. I need you to be brave. David was killed in a car accident. He had a heart attack while driving home from the boat." She was clearly in distraught even though she tried to sound calm for my sake.

> *What? David died? This must be a mistake! How could it be? He was very much alive last week, climbing up and down, adjusting the sail of the boat, fishing with Joe, taking us shopping in Vermont, and showing us around Montreal…*

"Noooo!" I screamed. "I've been trying to get hold of you the past few days. Nobody was picking up the phone, and I was getting worried. How could this happen?" I wept.

"I know, dear. You know he loved you very much and was very proud of you!"

"I love him too. He was like the father I never had. There was so much he wanted to teach me…"

"It's simply tragic. My life has been turned upside down because of it. I have a lot to take care of right now. I'll call you later, OK dear?" There was indescribable sadness in her voice.

"Please take care of yourself. I love you!"

"I love you, too!"

David came to my life like a beautiful flower, blossoming gloriously and disappearing so quickly. He was going to teach me how to start a business and find my way in this new Western world. He told me I could accomplish anything if I put my mind to it. Now I hoped more than ever that he was right.

\*

Most couples started their life together by planning a wedding. Joe and I skipped the wedding part and poured all our energy into getting me a visa to enter America so that we could live together. We thought the quickest way to obtain a visa would be to join him as a spouse. Joe initially hoped that I would manage to get a marriage certificate without him returning to Shanghai. It was not possible. In China, almost anything could be done through *guanxi* (connections). But at the age of twenty-one, my *guanxi* network was limited. And none of our families knew anyone working in the government with the authority to issue marriage certificates. So Joe made plans to fly back during his first summer break. Gjyn and Mitch had gone back to Australia and generously sent him a check to cover the airfare.

Nine months after Joe left for New York, I took the train to Beijing, the capital of China, and was reunited with the love of my life. The long separation made our time together even more precious and sweet. We vowed that from then on we would stay together for the rest of our lives. Joe and I had our little honeymoon in Beijing, climbing the Great Wall, visiting the Forbidden City, and boating on the Beidai River. We were inseparable and had the best times of our lives. I wished it could stay like this forever. But life was not honeymoon. There were hurdles to overcome and battles to fight in Shanghai.

Mr. Shen left a note for me to see him as soon as I got back on campus from Beijing. He worked in the English department without speaking any English. He was our political instructor who led us in the weekly political affair discussions, and also played a role as our career counselor. Mr. Shen was short and stout. His small eyes turned into two dots behind his glasses when he frowned. He had been pressuring me to become a member of the Communist Party for the last three years. Due to my religious belief, I had politely but repeatedly declined his invitations. He made me attend every new member meeting and always asked me to share my thoughts and feelings at the end of the meeting. I couldn't say I didn't want to join because I was a Christian. So I used the Chinese virtue of modesty to my advantage by saying that I didn't think I had quite met the high standard yet and would like to continue working on it. Mr. Shen got so concerned with my political wellbeing that he stopped by my home during my junior year to have a chat with Grandma. Towards the end of that strange conversation, he asked Grandma whether I had a boyfriend since he couldn't always find me on campus.

I loved Grandma's answer, which showed her witty side. "I don't know if Hongwei has a boyfriend. Boys come here and look for her all the time, but I don't know if she likes any of them."

Mr. Shen left my home empty-handed.

"How was your trip to Beijing?" Mr. Shen asked with a restrained smile when I sat down in his office with his note in my hand.

"It was great!" I was anxious to find out what he had in mind.

"Well, while you were gone, we had a staff meeting. Since you are one of the most outstanding students in the department, we all agreed that you should stay and become a staff member."

"But I don't want to be a teacher. I want to go to America," I disagreed feverishly.

"I know, I know. All we're asking from you is two years. Teach here for two years, and we'll give you the green light to go abroad."

"But I don't want to wait for two years," I muttered.

"Well, no matter where you go, you'll be required a two-year service period. It's the policy. There's no way around it." He frowned.

It felt like I just hit a wall. I was close to tears.

"Talk to Joe and make your future plans accordingly. It's an honor to be offered the staff position. The decision is final." With that, he concluded the conversation, leaving me in despair.

*This whole thing doesn't feel like an honor, but imprisonment!*

I went to the department dean. He was an older guy who looked like Deng Xiaoping. Mr. Dean gave people the impression that his words and thoughts didn't always go together. It was hard to read him.

He told me bluntly, "I can't override the decision made by the staff. Everyone wanted you, and you'll have to stay."

Joe and I discussed my limited options. We knew about the two-year service policy. My only chance to get around it would be to seek employment from privately owned or preferably joint venture firms. But now I was forced to stay and teach for at least two years. We absolutely didn't want to live thousands of miles away from each other again!

At the time, Mr. Chen was the president of East China University of Science and Technology. He was relatively young, in his late forties and a self-proclaimed reformer. In his most recent speech, he claimed that the top students in the university should be given the freedom to choose their career instead of being assigned.

"According to Mr. Chen, I should be able to choose where I want to go," I said to Joe.

"Then it looks like you need to go and talk to the president."

"It never hurts to ask, right?"

"You are right about that, baby." Joe winked at me.

The next day I walked into the president's office. He wasn't there, and so I talked to his secretary about my situation and my desire to seek employment outside the university. She took notes and promised that she would deliver the message.

Mr. Shen's tone softened the next time we discussed my assignment.

"We still want you to stay. But if it's something you absolutely don't want to do, it is OK with me. But you'll have to get approval from the dean. I am OK if he is OK with it."

*Whoa-la! There is an opening. The secretary must have delivered the message!*

Joe and I went to the dean's home that night to persuade him in person. He couldn't understand why we were so desperate to be together and why I would throw away a bright future to go to America. After about thirty minutes, he and Joe were basically repeating the same lines over and over. The dean was in his early sixties and appeared exhausted after his bedtime. In the end, he compromised just to get rid of us.

"Okay. If you want to find a different job, go ahead and do that. But I am telling you, you are walking away from a great opportunity. I hope you'll think it through."

There was nothing to think through. I wanted to go to America with Joe. But who would hire me and let me off the hook immediately? My excitement was quickly overshadowed by the bigger challenges ahead.

One of Joe's relatives worked in the personnel department of a joint venture company. I was hopeful he would help me out. But he thought it would impact his career negatively if his boss hired me based on his recommendation, and I turned around and requested permission to leave the company immediately.

So I went job hunting on my own and applied for an executive administrative assistant position at Johnson & Johnson

Company in Shanghai and was offered the job on the spot. The human source manager Ms. Wu seemed kind and approachable. I went back to her a couple of days later.

Ms. Wu shared a big office with a number of her colleagues. Her desk was the neatest and she the most pleasant.

"Nice to see you again, Ms. Wu!"

"Oh, hi!" She was a little surprised to see me. "What can I do for you?"

"I—I am getting married. Could you provide me with the paperwork to obtain the marriage certificate?" I said softly, trying not to draw attention from her colleagues.

She looked me up and down, then her eyes stopped at the middle. "Are you pregnant?"

"No, I am not pregnant. My fiancé studies overseas. He is back in Shanghai but will have to leave again soon. We want to get married."

"Ooh, in that case, no problem. Which country is he studying at?"

"America. Well, here's the thing, after we get married I want to go with him to America. I'll also need the documents to apply for the passport and visa." My voice was reduced to a whisper. I was prepared for a strong reaction any moment.

"You want to go to America? But you employment hasn't started yet. Oh, my! I don't know about that." Instead of raising her voice, she lowered it too.

"I actually don't need this job. But without an employer, I can't get all the required rubber-stamped documents to get a passport. I don't know what to do. Could you help me out?"

She thought for a minute, before she answered, "Let me go talk to my boss. But I'm pretty sure she won't like it."

Ms. Wu left and after a while came back with a younger woman by her side. This woman wore gold-framed glasses and had lots of freckles on her stern-looking face.

"This is Director Liu. I just talked to her about your situation." Ms. Wu smiled nervously at her boss and then at me.

"Nice to meet you!" I extended my hand.

She took it expressionlessly. "Ms. Wu told me that you wanted to get married and go to America. Since you haven't even started working here, we can't provide you with the paperwork for your passport. I advise you to work hard and prove yourself before asking for anything." She walked away indignantly. All the eyes in the office glared at me and the only thing I could do was put my head down to avoid eye contact.

"If she doesn't approve, I'm afraid there is nothing I can do." Ms. Wu forced an awkward smile.

*This is bad. I just escaped from one trap only to get into another!*

Since Ms. Wu was my only connection to Johnson & Johnson, I had no choice but win her over. Joe and I invited her out for coffee. She was curious about what life was like in America. Joe filled her in with detailed and vivid descriptions. Ms. Wu really had a soft spot. She told us her only son died of leukemia when he was only seven. To this day, she still felt guilty about it. As she put it, "How can all the other mothers raise healthy children but I failed?"

I could feel her agony and pain. As we talked, she was able to feel my frustration of possibly being separated again from the man I wanted to spend the rest of my life with. "I really want to help you. But my hands are tied. You know how Ms. Liu is like." She gave out a big sigh and began to examine her fingernails.

After a few seconds of dead silence, her face lit up. "Unless, unless you talk to the general manager, your future boss, directly."

"You think he'd he give me the green light?"

"I'm not sure. But he's from Taiwan and educated in the U.S. He is a lot more open-minded and empathetic especially with things of this nature. It's worth a try."

"How can I meet him?" My heart raced at the first sign of hope in days.

"He travels a lot and isn't in the office that much. But he'll be back next Tuesday. How about you show up next Tuesday morning and ask to see him?"

"Okay. Great! What should I say?"

Ms. Wu suggested a brilliant dialogue that could possibly get me the documents necessary to exit the country. Joe and I were elated.

On Tuesday morning, I arrived in Ms. Wu's office wearing a fitted red silk dress with small white polka dots. My shoulder-length hair was pulled straight with my bangs slightly above my eyebrows. I was nervous because this would be the make it or break it moment.

"He's here. I'll take you to his office," Ms. Wu whispered and looked a little uneasy.

We walked silently through the hallway that led to the big boss's office. The only sound that could be heard was our heels in contact with the tile floor. If this didn't go well, it could put Ms. Wu at odds with her boss. I absolutely didn't want that to happen.

The door to the general manager's office was open. He sat behind a large high-end cherry wood desk.

"Hi, Mr. Koh!" Ms. Wu bowed humbly. "This is your new assistant, Linda. She wants to discuss some personal matters with you."

He looked up and waved to me. "Come on in and sit down."

Mr. Koh was a big man with a snub meaty nose, slanted eyes, and a smile like Buddha.

I walked in and sat across from him. Ms. Wu excused herself and closed the door. Behind Mr. Koh on the credenza were pictures of his adorable family.

"You have a wonderful family," I commented admiringly.

"Thank you!" He turned around, pointed at one of the pictures and smiled proudly. "This is Emily; she is seven. And this is Emma, and she is four."

"They are adorable!"

"Oh, thank you very much!" Mr. Koh struck me as a family man. "So, tell me what you want to discuss."

"Well, my fiancé is studying for a Ph.D. in New York. He is back in Shanghai right now, and we are getting married."

"Congratulations! That's great!"

I cleared my throat and smiled at him nervously. "I'd love to go to America for our honeymoon. I know I haven't started my job yet, and I am already asking for a vacation. Would you be OK with that?"

"Am I OK with that? Absolutely!"

My heart pounded so fiercely in my chest that I could hear it. "Thank you, Mr. Koh! In that case, I need the official documents with the Johnson & Johnson rubberstamp in order to apply for the passport and visa."

"I don't see any problem with that. I'll ask Ms. Liu to get them for you."

He called Ms. Liu on the intercom and there was a knock on the door within a few minutes.

"Come in," Mr. Koh shouted to the door.

Ms. Liu stepped in cautiously, shocked to see me there.

"Ms. Liu. This is Linda. Have you two met before?"

"Yes, we have." Ms. Liu forced a smile.

"Linda is getting married. She plans to go to America for her honeymoon. Isn't that great?" Mr. Koh gave out a hearty laugh.

Ms. Liu followed with a hollow cackle.

"Could you get Linda all the paperwork she needs for her passport?"

Ms. Liu blushed and then grew pale by turns. She wanted to say something, but bit her tongue. "Yes, of course. I'll get everything ready for her."

For a brief moment, I felt sorry for putting Ms. Liu in such a conflicting position.

I got up from my chair. "Thank you so much, Mr. Koh. I really appreciate it!" I was over the moon.

He shook my hand and gave it a squeeze. "Again congratulations!"

I had barely reached the door when I heard him calling me, "Hey, Linda …"

"Yeah?" I turned around.

"If you ever decide to come back, the job will be here for you for a year."

"Terrific! Thank you again!"

Within a couple of hours, I got all the necessary documents. I was on my way to America, my new home with Joe! Joe and I decided to host a farewell dinner before he had to leave. In my mind it was also a dress-down version of a wedding banquet. I went to my parents to extend the invitation.

"Joe is leaving next week. We are hosting a dinner party this Saturday. We'd like you to come," I started enthusiastically.

They had this gloomy look on their faces like I just told them someone had died. My father's condition had rapidly worsened after retirement. The hot and humid summer and cold and damp winter in Shanghai were not kind to his eczema. He breathed heavily, constantly gasping for air. Father pretty much did nothing all day but sit in the same bamboo couch brought back from Yun Nan watching TV or napping. Occasionally, he would ask my mother to take out his favorite suit from the wardrobe and brag about its high quality. It was custom-made centuries ago by the best tailor in Shanghai just for him.

"Well, I don't like to be in an air-conditioned room with lots of people. I won't be able breathe. Maybe your mother can go."

"Okay, I'll go," Mother said reluctantly as if she was doing me a favor.

My mother came to the party wearing a strained smile all night. It was painful to watch her. I couldn't understand why my parents just couldn't be happy for me.

In mid-September, a couple of weeks after Joe returned to New York, I went to the U.S. Consulate in Shanghai early in the morning before it opened. The line was already miles long wrapping around the fenced walls. Just being able to make this line was a tremendous achievement. Everyone had a story to tell. People were chatting loudly about their friends whose visa applications got rejected, the circumstances, and those who were approved. There were lots of older people in line trying to go to America to visit their children. Since most schools in the U.S. had already been in session, only a few young people were there, hoping to get the student visa. Then there were people like me who planned to join their spouses and also a handful of applicants traveling for business.

The level of anxiety and anticipation was unbelievable as if this were the defining moment of our lives, like we were standing at the gate that would open to a far better and more promising world. Getting the visa would be the only way to cross the gate.

The door finally opened and a few people were let in at a time. The expression on their faces when they came out showed without a shadow of doubt as to the person's approval or rejection.

It was my turn after what seemed like a lifelong wait. I clenched the envelope that contained all the information I might be asked to present. My hands were shaking. Even though they typically didn't reject spouses, it had been a rough morning for most of the people ahead of me.

I was motioned to go to an open window. The Caucasian man standing behind the window wore small-framed glasses. He was skinny, tall, and had a pointy nose.

"Who are you going to visit?" He asked while looking at my application.

"My husband."

"What's he doing in the U.S.?"

"Pursing a Ph.D. degree in physics."

He turned his eyes from the paper to me. "How long have you been married?"

"We just got married." I regretted being so eager the minute these words came out of my mouth.

"Can you show me your marriage certificate?"

"Umm, sorry, I might have forgotten to bring it with me," I stammered, fumbling through the envelope as if I were looking for that piece of paper.

"I can't issue you a visa without taking a look at the proof of your marriage. You'll have to come back another day." He jotted down something at the back of my passport and yelled, "Next!"

I couldn't show him the marriage certificate in the envelope because it stated that I was married two years ago. Joe and I had heard rumors that there was a new policy that required couples to be married for at least two years before one could join the other. So with gifts and *guanxi,* we managed to have the clerk write 1986 instead of 1988 on my certificate.

> *Oh, bummer! I was so close to getting the license to cross the gate. I should have said we had gotten our marriage certificate two years ago but had our wedding ceremony recently.*

I had to explain the situation to the same clerk several times before he consented grudgingly to change the date to what it should have been. I returned to the consulate the next day, hoping it would be smooth sailing. It was the same mile-long line, loud chatting, and agonizing wait. Then it was my turn.

The guard flipped my passport to the last page and bellowed, "You can't go in."

"Why? I was here yesterday, and he told me to come back."

"He wrote '1 year' on the last page, which means you can't apply again until after a year." He literally shoved me aside so that others could come forward.

"It was that tall American who told me to come back. Could you go and ask him?" I begged.

The guard ignored me completely and went about his business checking other people's passports. I wanted to scream but felt too disgusted to do so. I was totally drained. Was it an innocent mistake or did the tall guy do it on purpose? I'd never find out, and it didn't matter because I would be stuck here for another year. I wandered aimlessly on the street, feeling trapped, helpless and homeless.

*Where am I going to live and what am I going to do for a whole year?*

I had graduated and therefore could no longer go back to my little dorm room. My parents had retired just before I left home for college and now lived in that little room at 930 Long. My mother would ask my sister to call me and ask me to go home for the weekend. But there was no place for me to sleep. My father and sister took the two twin beds. My mother slept on the couch, and I spent the night on my father's bamboo chair and woke up sore and unrested. There was no way I'd live with my parents. Grandma was still with Aunt and Yan, and I had stayed there for the last few weeks but a year would be a different story. Joe and I spent the last three months in a semi-furnished apartment in Pudong that belonged to his sister Meihua and brother-in-law. Even if I could still live there, it would be awfully lonely without Joe and it was too far away from the city.

*Do I go back to Johnson & Johnson and ask for my job back? No, I don't want to see that freckled Ms. Liu again. How can I possibly have any* guanxi *to get back into the consulate behind the iron gate? Who can get me back in? Who? Who? Who?*

The light bulb lit up in my head. Ed and Carol were my English teachers from America. I had been having Bible study with them since Gjyn and Mitch left. I wasn't as close to them as I was to Gjyn and Mitch. Ed and Carol were quieter and more reserved. They mentioned once about having dinner with the consul general. It wouldn't hurt to ask.

I got on the bus and headed to their apartment in the same building where Gjyn and Mitch used to live. Carol answered the door. She was taller than her husband, which was unusual to the Chinese. They had two cute little girls.

I could no longer hold back my tears. There was a pile of tissues on the coffee table by the time I finished telling them the story. Carol rubbed my hand empathetically while Ed listened quietly with a thoughtful look on his face.

"Linda, we usually don't do this. But this sounds like a mistake. Let me make a call." Ed stood up and left the room.

In a few minutes Ed came back with a grin on his face. "I'll go with you to the consulate tomorrow morning!"

"Really, you'll do that for me? You don't know how much it means to me!"

"Promise me you won't tell anyone about this. We can't help everyone who wants to go to America."

"Promise!" It almost felt like I was given a second chance at life.

Very early next morning in the torrential rain, I arrived at the consulate the third time in a week. Ed came shortly afterwards in a transparent raincoat and stood by the gate. When I approached the gate, Ed whispered to the guard who in turn nodded. I went inside and Ed waited in the guard's little booth by the gate.

I waited until the tall guy became available and went up to his window.

"I was here a couple of days ago. I forgot to bring my marriage certificate. I have it with me today." I handed him the certificate with the red silk cover.

He looked at it carefully. "Why is it there are two dates on this thing?"

"The handwritten one that says 1988 is the correct date. There is a stamp next to it to validate the correction." Never a good liar, I had to make it sound as truthful as possible. My heart skipped a few beats in the process.

He paused for a few seconds, and then with a smile declared "Okay then. Enjoy your visit to the U.S."

*Yes!*

"Thank you!" I heaved a big sigh of relief.

The middle-aged woman ahead of me in line also got a visa to visit her husband. We walked out together giggling. There was construction going on inside the consulate compound. Out of nowhere a piece of wood board flew into the air in the stormy wind. She pulled me aside. "Be careful, we are worth much more now. We'd better take good care of ourselves."

I laughed.

*She is right. Yesterday I had no idea where I was going. Today I am going home!*

Ed came out of the Guard's booth to meet me.

"I got it! I got it!" I waved the envelope with my passport inside excitedly.

Ed grinned from ear to ear.

"Did he apologize?" Ed asked.

"Apologize? Why apologize? To whom?"

"To you for mistakenly writing '1 yr' at the back of your passport."

"No, he didn't apologize, and he didn't have to," I giggled.

Ed shook his head.

\*

I was so happy when Lin called one day almost a year after I left Living Water to invite me to have regular fellowship with her and Charlotte. I offered my basement. They soon became my link to Living Water since I learned the major events and the coming and going of people through them.

Lin was a mathematics professor of a private college, and she also managed to teach Sunday school, go on mission trips, and take theological classes all at the same time. Amazing woman! During the fellowship in my basement, she frequently shared God's amazing work through her mission trips as well as what she was learning at Trinity Christian College.

"I've never realized how truly amazing the Bible is. Everything is intricately connected. Many prophecies are hidden in the old testaments and fulfilled and revealed in vivid details in later chapters. It's like God's hands are weaving through the whole book and the whole human history. Now even reading Jesus' genealogy moves me to tears since behind every name, there is a miraculous story that speaks of God's salvation and deliverance." Lin spoke with such conviction and passion. Growing up in Beijing, her Mandarin was perfect, and she ended the last word of every sentence with a curl. This was what I loved about Lin: conviction, passion, and expression.

Our conversations were not limited to spiritual topics. The small and intimate setting allowed us to connect at a more personal level.

"Lin, what is it like to be a pastor's wife?" I asked one day. Her husband used to be an IT professional and a member of Living Water, now its assistant pastor.

"It's different from being a regular church member, that's for sure. Grant is playing a very different role, which changes things for me as well."

Even before Grant became the assistant pastor of Living Water, they were key members of the church. They started the Peter's Fellowship targeting Mainland Chinese. In the beginning only a handful people attended the once-a-month gathering. With the increase of the Asian population in Naperville, Peter's fellowship grew as well. After Rev. Zhong joined Living Water as its senior pastor, he put a lot of focus on Peter's Fellowship by offering special talks and organizing fun activities. Peter's Fellowship grew in leaps and bounds from a handful to more than a dozen small groups. Grant and Lin planted the seeds and set it on the right course because they had a vision. Both of them had served on the BOD, and Grant was also heavily involved in worship team as he was a talented musician who played violin and erhu competently.

"What's the biggest difference between being a member and being the wife of the pastor?" Charlotte followed up.

"It has to be that I no longer have a voice." Lin grew thoughtful and serious.

Charlotte and I burst into laughter because we thought she was joking.

"I am not kidding! It's a serious matter not to have a voice!" Lin blushed.

It suddenly dawned on me that she wasn't pulling our legs. Lin was a thinker and eloquent speaker. She wasn't shy of being heard when I served on the BOD with her. But to support her husband's ministry and maintain the unity of the church, she had to learn to tune down her opinions in order not to rock the boat. It must have been a daunting adjustment!

Charlotte was going through what appeared to be an amicable divorce. If there was much internal turmoil, she managed to put forward a strong front. She was a professor of family and child studies. Charlotte was articulate, a good listener, and always provided good invited insight, a rare quality in the first-generation Chinese immigrant community. She had a distinctive laugh: when she laughed, every part of her body participated.

One Thursday night Lin and Charlotte came to my house in the subzero Chicago weather. Inside I felt just as cold. Joe and I hadn't spoken to each other for four days. I had sent him a desperate email saying how unhappy I had become and how I didn't see any hope of us ever making each other happy again. He didn't respond and simply came home with a grave look on his face. After all these years, he was still capable of stabbing me in the heart by his silence.

I let the ladies in and the three of us went down to one of the two bigger rooms in the basement. Each of us took our usual spot: Lin and Charlotte on the blue and cream-colored sofa, and I perched on the denim beanbag chair across from them. On the coffee table, I had prepared hot drinks, fruits, and snacks.

Lin came directly from school, and she wore a pink turtleneck inside a dark red and black blazer. Charlotte was in a pink sweater with a silk scarf tied around her neck. Our conversation was pretty much the same: Lin shared her new spiritual insight, we talked about our children, our jobs, the people who were sick and needed prayer …

Charlotte mentioned that her ex had purchased a new house and was about to move out, which would be another painful milestone in this process. It was the first time I sensed the distress caused by her divorce. A couple of times, I was about to tell them that things didn't look good for Joe and me and we were on the verge of getting a divorce, but each time I held back. We prayed for each other at the end. Lin and Charlotte always remembered to pray for Joe, the prodigal son, that one day would go back to his father again. I prayed for peace and wisdom.

When they left, I went to the study where Joe had been spending most of his time after work.

"Can we talk?" I demanded in a stony voice.

"Okay." He didn't even look up.

We went to our bedroom on the first floor and shut the door.

"Why are you not talking to me?" I wanted to kill him.

"What do you want me to say? If you tell me specifically what I can do to make you happy, I'll do it. What am I supposed to do when you say something like if things don't change, you won't be able to stick around much longer? Is that a threat?"

"Are you happy with the way we are?" My voice turned pitchy.

"It's OK."

"But it's not OK for me. This is killing me. I can't live like this!"

"So what do you want to do?"

I grew quiet, weeping without tears. "We can't make each other happy. Maybe we shouldn't be together anymore. You may be able to find someone who can appreciate your active mind and critical thinking."

"So you don't love me anymore. Is that it?" he roared.

"I don't know. I am not sure about anything anymore."

"So you want a divorce? Okay, fine! What are we going to do about Jake?"

"If we split, I want to go back to China. I can teach English, and I'll take Jake with me. You can visit him or he can spend the summer with you."

Joe's face fell, his voice cracking.

"Why are you doing this to me? Why are you doing this to Jake?"

"It's because we can't agree on the most important things in life, the things that define who we are." I could no longer hold back my tears.

"Do you love me or do you love me for God?"

I had asked myself that question over and over again in the past three years, but I still didn't have the answer.

"I don't know. I think I still love you, but I really don't know," I sobbed.

Joe pulled me to him, and we hugged. I melted in his arms. We made love, intense, passionate love, the best of its sort. A big chunk of negative energy was released from my body. But both he and I knew that the issue hadn't been resolved. It would come back to haunt us again and again until I had the answer to his question "Do you love me or do you love me for God?"

\*

"If you are this unhappy, then maybe you should leave!" Joe uttered the ultimatum as we were lying in bed one night trying to have a constructive discussion.

My heart skipped a beat. This was the first time he had ever asked me to get out since we were married. Joe and I had been engaged in this vicious and tacit cycle: he wanted me to profess my unconditional love towards him, and I wanted him to believe in God again without me making him. Both of us knew that things of that nature couldn't be forced. So instead we picked at each other over every other little thing.

I hit another low a few days ago when Joe and I had a disagreement about Jake and talked myself into believing that things weren't going to work out between us. We were too different. This was all too consuming and maybe not worth it in the end. I wanted out. I wanted to run away.

*Divorce will be hard on everyone. But it will be short-term versus life-long pain. Jane and Michelle have passed the vulnerable age, and hopefully they will get over it. Jake is not five yet. He needs both his mommy and daddy to love him and care for him. This is the hard part. Things would have been so much easier if we didn't have Jake. I can just go and explore the world on my own. I married too young and have never really got the opportunity to be on my own.*

The minute I realized that I was actually fancying a life without Jake, I knew I had hit bottom. Immediately a swarm of images and fond memories of little Jake began whirling in my head: his little fists, his giggle, his first step, his first tooth. He was the reason I had managed to hold together in the last three years. He was why I still laughed everyday. He was my motivation to continue fighting and not give up.

Growing up, I had always been an annoyance, an unwanted body in a crowded space. I was never going to allow my children to feel like that. They were precious and meant the whole world to me. They were worth fighting for. The thing with hitting the bottom was that you either stay there and rot—or you climb back up. The choice was obvious.

I thought it was time to have a serious talk with Joe about our children, our future, and us.

"You know, I've been struggling for almost three years. It's been difficult and painful." I thought it would be wise to start with the "I" statements.

"You are struggling, you are unhappy, you are miserable. Why is everything always about you? Have you ever considered my feelings?"

The hell with the "I" statements! "If I can't tell you I am unhappy, who am I going to tell?"

"All I want is for you to be happy. When you are happy, everything is wonderful. You can make me so happy too," Joe's tone softened a bit.

"If I know how to be happy, we don't have a problem anymore, right? But I don't know, not anymore!"

"If you are this unhappy, then leave!" His words were like a door slamming in my face.

I went silent.

*Is it too late for us to make it work? Has the warmth completely gone out of our marriage?*

"This is my home. You leave!" I said calmly but firmly, preparing myself for what was going to happen next.

Long pause. Time seemed to freeze. Then he heaved a big sigh. "Just tell me, what can I do to make you happy?"

*Okay, he didn't leave. That's a good sign.*

"I want you to stop trying to make me happy and feeling defeated when you can't. The truth is only I can make me happy. And I am going to work on it." I was waiting for Joe to jump in with a long lecture, but he didn't. So I continued, "I want you to be a good listener instead of always lecturing me on what to do. I want you to be my husband instead of my father. I needed a father at sixteen, but I am a grown woman now and should be treated like one."

"Okay. That's good, that's good. So how are you going to be happy?"

"I don't know yet. But I'll figure it out. I'll ask for your help when I need it."

"Do you still love me?" There was tenderness and eagerness in his voice.

"Yup!"

"Are you sure?"

"Yup!"

"I love you, but I hate you, too." Joe turned me to face him.

I actually wasn't one hundred percent sure but sure enough to say yes. I had decided it would be the best to fall in love with the same man I married to, for my sake, for our children's sake, and for Joe's as well. The part in me that was unsure, I'd just have to bring it to fall in love again so that it would be in harmony with the other bigger part that was sure.

*All I need to do is fall in love and be happy—the ongoing quest of mankind. Now that I have a clear goal in mind, I think it can be done.*

\*

For three years I refused to even look at what Joe was reading. Now I accepted his invitation to read a few books. I read *The Science of Happiness* by Stephan Klein and *The Astonishing Hypothesis: The Scientific Search for the Soul* by Francis Crick. I also watched the Kitzmiller vs. Dover Area School District bench trial, the first trial in the federal courts against a school district that mandated the teaching of intelligent design. It was all very interesting and intriguing. My mind was shifting.

I shared with Lin and Charlotte that I had seriously contemplated divorce but had decided to make my marriage work for the sake of my family. They were shocked about the divorce part. I mentioned some of the books I was reading. Lin was concerned that these books may lead me in the wrong direction.

"If Eve could be tempted, who are we to assume that we won't be?" Lin believed strongly that we should only immerse ourselves in God's word.

"It's good that she is exploring. I don't think it's harmful at all," Charlotte commented.

Charlotte had recommended Dr. Harriet Lerner's books to me. I read all of them and conceded that I had to deal with my anger issues at a deeper level. I wrote to Dr. Lerner about my marital difficulties. She encouraged me not to give up because it was worth saving.

For a while I kept my mind shifting about God mostly to myself since it was such an intimate and emotional thing. One day when Lin went on and on about how flawless the Bible was, it just came out.

"I've started to have doubts about the Bible," I stated uneasily.

"Really?" Lin sounded alarmed.

"Take Noah's ark for example. According to an article recently published by *Nature*, the number of species on earth is now estimated at 8.7 million. The dimensions given in the Bible can calculate the size of the ark. How could all these species fit in that boat?"

"God has his miraculous ways of doing things." I expected Lin to say that.

"But it has to make sense. Plus there is no scientific evidence that there has ever been a global flood that wiped out everything."

"Science can't validate everything."

"If evolution is correct, from all I have read, I think it is. It does cast serious doubts about the biblical description of how humans were created."

"But Linda, the Bible is true in so many ways. Do you have to focus your attention on a few places, namely the first chapter of the book?"

"But my problem is with the claim that the Bible is impeccable, and that every word is the truth. If I can poke a hole in one place, I am no longer confident that the rest is that impeccable."

"So where do you stand right now?" Charlotte jumped in.

"That the God as described in the Bible may not be real."

Lin grew silent with a serious and saddened look on her face, "It's the season of life. You and Joe are in a different season right now. But both of you are chosen by God. He won't give up on you. He will leave the ninety-nine sheep aside to find that lost one. I am sure about that."

Something changed that moment. Sides had been taken. I sensed that things would never be the same again for Lin and me. She would continue to pray for Joe and me ceaselessly and compassionately for as long as it would take and I'd rush to her side immediately if she ever needed me, but we wouldn't be having our basement connections for much longer. I'd always treasure the deep bonding Lin and I shared in Christ, but now I had to let it go because a fundamental change had occurred.

# Let Go

Sitting in front of the traffic light waiting for that green arrow, I wondered why I had always felt safer being prompted to make the left turn. Why was it that all my life I had been looking for signs and permission to do things properly?

God had been my green arrow: he instructed me what I ought to do and what I should stay away from. I followed diligently and faithfully, hoping that in turn I would be blessed with an abundant eternal life, constantly apprehensive that I wasn't reading the Bible enough, or praying enough to stay connected with him, not loving others enough to deserve his love, not humble enough in the face of his glory, and generally not good enough to be chosen by him.

> *Now that I am breaking away from God, can I make it on my own? Can I make the left turn without the green arrow? Who am I? How do I relate to others? If I am no longer doing everything to please him, who do I please? What is the purpose and meaning of my life? What do I do with the time and energy used to be devoted to serving God? What happens to me after I die?*

Like someone who was involved in a car accident and sustained brain damage, I had to re-learn how to talk, walk, and think. I had to figure out the answers to so many questions that I used to have the clear-cut answers.

Initially whenever Living Water made an effort to reconnect with me, I responded positively and graciously. All I needed was an invitation. So upon invitation, I returned to perform an on-stage sermon translation as well as coordinate the vow renewal ceremony. What I found was that serving God and the church without a solid faith was confusing and strenuous. So I disappeared again after the jobs were done.

For years I had presented the Christ-like part of me to the church, and they had accepted me as one of them. But nobody knew how to handle the other side of me that was doubtful, cynical, and wounded. So I was left alone to deal with my own problems and restore my faith. What separated them and me was more than the distance between Living Water and the Compass Church, but who I really was. The fundamental question was whether I was one of them or one of the world.

I was excited when some old friends from one of the small groups under Peter's Fellowship, of which Joe and I used to be key members, invited us to join their monthly gatherings. This group, known as Peace, had grown into a few groups by that time, and the original members launched a monthly fellowship to stay in touch with one another. I thought we would have a much better chance of reconnecting with the old friends in a sociable environment. But it turned out to be a false assumption.

The main agenda of the monthly meeting was actually for half of the original Peace members who were committed Christians to win back the other half who had ceased going to church and growing spiritually. Joe happened to be in China the first time I went. It was an absolute joy to see more than a dozen familiar faces. The connection was warm and instant. After dinner, we gathered around the dining room table to discuss the topic of the evening: our New Year's resolution in spiritual terms.

"I'll really try to read the Bible more and on a daily basis. I've been out of a job for over a year and thought I'd have so much more time. But somehow so many other things quickly fill my day," Leah, a realtor in training, reflected.

"I'll serve God more in the New Year. God saved me from a major car collision last month. My car was totaled, but, miraculously, I survived with a scratch. I'll serve him with a more willing and humble heart," Mia, already a devoted church volunteer, spoke with profound gratefulness.

The other half of the room took their turns with less demonstrated zeal.

"You're all so spiritual. I don't know what to say after you guys. Well, I'll try to take better care of my family and myself in the new year," Ming commented with a blush.

"I'll be kinder and more forgiving because that will improve my relationships with others," Jane, whose hobby was acting, said thoughtfully, twirling her long hair.

Sitting at the end of the table, I listened quietly while trying to form the sentences in my head. A couple of years ago I would have said with passion and determination something like I'd strive to build a God-centered home. But it wouldn't sound genuine right now. "I don't really have any New Year resolutions. I'll just see where life takes me. I used to be very spiritual." I glanced at the left side of the table. "But I am not any more. Joe has given up his faith, and I am struggling. For a while, I didn't even know whether I still loved him. But he's the love of my life and always will be. We are having open discussions again and I am rethinking through things I used to believe I had already known the answers." I paused to get a feel for the reactions from the table.

Bella from the right side of the table jumped in. "I admire your courage. You're actually more real and lovable than you've ever been before."

I smiled at her.

I left the gathering feeling good and accepted. This was the first time I had ever shared my spiritual battles publicly. I was looking forward to rejoining the group soon.

\*

Things began to change when Joe entered the scene and took the center stage of discussion. I was talking to the ladies when I heard him speaking loudly and authoritatively about evolution in the dining room with the guys. I went into the dining room and gently put my hands on his shoulders. He looked up and smiled. I squinted and shook my head slightly.

"It's OK. They are our old friends. We're just having an interesting conversation." Joe was excited to have an audience.

"Let him talk. It's OK," Mia's husband Lee said with a grin.

I gave Joe's shoulders a little squeeze and returned to my own uncontroversial chat.

We watched a familiar evangelical DVD after dinner. The author painstakingly tried to attribute the chaotic five thousand years of Chinese history with all its self-destruction, misery, oppression, and ruin to the lack of reverence for God. He also attempted to make a connection between some of the Chinese philosophers such as Lao Zi and Confucius to the Bible prophecies, indicating that God was speaking to the Chinese thousands of years ago through these philosophers.

"So what do you think of it?" Leah smiled charmingly as she looked around the table.

Before anyone had a chance to comment, Joe blurted out, "It's total nonsense. The connection between the Chinese philosophers and the Bible is farfetched and imaginary. The Bible never hints in any way that Lao Zi and Confucius are prophets sent by God to the Chinese."

For a second the room went mum, everyone looked at each other in surprise and smiled politely, especially the ladies who weren't involved in the earlier discussion. This wasn't going to be a dull dialogue if one didn't mind listening to Joe for the rest of the evening. Because from that point on, he dominated the discussion by going on and on about the evolution theories and how his study of the brain led him to believe that our need for God was genetically coded in our brain as a result of evolution. As he talked, the bewilderment deepened. The people in the room were used to the old Joe who was on the other side of the fence defending God's word and the truthfulness of the Bible.

Around ten o'clock, I whispered to Joe that we should leave. We had left Jake under the care of Michelle for almost five hours, and I felt the room had more than enough dosage of shock for the day.

"It's good to see you again, Joe. It was an interesting discussion. Thanks for sharing with us openly," Mia sent us off with kind remarks.

"Next time could you give other people a chance to talk as well? When you are the only one talking, it becomes a lecture not a conversation," I said to Joe once we got into the car.

"Sure, sure! I bet some of them have never thought about religion and God this way before, I really got them thinking." Joe was obviously satisfied about getting it off his chest.

Contrary to Joe's self-indulgence, the group became less tolerant of his lectures, and things got a bit more heated every time. Even the other half of the room who had been idle with God insisted that there had to be a God in charge of the universe and our eternity.

"God is so powerful, and in front of him, we are like little babies. God reveals to us what we can understand, just like you wouldn't teach Jake advanced physics because he's only five years old. There are so many things we can't understand, that is why faith is believing without seeing," Mia's husband Lee spoke earnestly.

"But science has advanced enough for us to ask intelligent questions about the accuracy of the Bible." Joe was fully charged for a new round of debate.

"But science is so limited. Its conclusions can change over time. But the Bible has been there for thousands of years and it hasn't and will never change," Lee pushed back.

"People used to believe that the earth was flat. Even the Bible described the earth as having four corners. Now we know it's a sphere. Using scientific methodology, we can estimate its size and age. There may still be arguments about whether it is a perfect sphere or slightly oval, but we know for sure it isn't flat, and that isn't going to change."

The room was getting nosier with more than one person talking. So Joe raised his voice. "Do you know what happens when you die? I've fully understood death, and I can face it with a smile on my face. And I know where I'm going after death."

"Tell us where you are going," Derek, Leah's husband, asked with his face turning red from the excitement.

"Heaven!"

"But didn't you say there was no heaven?" Derek roared with laughter.

Seeing that this discussion was going nowhere and the people around me were getting emotional, I intervened.

"You guys talk to him like he were a first time seeker. But Joe was a Christian like you. He has changed his mind after his brother's death and after examining many aspects of science and religion. You are not really talking to each other but over each other. It's getting late. We should go." I glanced at Joe.

Joe reluctantly stood up. "Yeah, sorry guys for talking so much. But this is important. We'll discuss more next time."

"Thank you, Joe, for your honest sharing. It's good to get together and have discussions like this." Mia was such a good sport.

"Joe, there is a God. There has to be. Don't be too arrogant," Bill, Bella's husband and the quiet guy in the crowd, whispered to Joe at the door when we were putting on our shoes.

"Why do you keep on doing this? I told you to cool it." I was ticked off.

"They started it by challenging me with evolutional questions right before dinner."

"And you have to react so strongly and turn it into a full-fledged debate? You used to be much more reserved and thoughtful. What happened to you?"

"It's OK. I am just speaking my mind among some old friends. Don't be mad at me, OK, baby?" He reached for my hand with a guilty smile.

I sighed.

*This is what I have to fall in love with again. It's not going to be easy, but throughout the years, Joe has loved and accepted me unconditionally. Maybe I should overlook his flaws the same way he has overlooked so many of mine.*

"I'm not mad at you. Do you know that I am the only one in this world who can understand you and accept you right now?"

"I know. That's why I love you so much!"

Leah called early Monday morning. "How are you doing? How is Joe?"

"Good. I am sorry he was so forceful and inconsiderate on Saturday."

"Yeah. He pretty much took over the discussion and nobody else got a chance to voice their opinion."

"Don't worry. He won't be going to the gatherings anymore."

"That's probably for the best."

I realized that Joe just got disinvited from a Bible study fellowship.

"Uh, I'll come whenever I can. But you don't need to check with my schedule anymore."

"We'd still love to have you, though."

"I'll try." I knew I was not going either.

Were the friends we had made through church only good when we shared the same faith? If that was the case, we needed new friends whom Joe could relate to in a different way.

*

Making new friends at this stage of our life would have been more difficult without Jake. Not too long after his fifth birthday, I found a white envelope in his cubby at the daycare. Inside was a birthday invitation card with handwriting on all sides except the cover. It was from Andy's mom Julia. She wrote how Andy had been talking about Jake constantly at home and how thrilled he would be if Jake could go to his birthday party. Jake's teacher, Ms. Rhonda, had told me that Jake took it upon himself to be Andy's buddy when he first joined the class. Jake lifted Andy's hand at lunchtime to show him how to request seconds and stuck up for Andy when some kids got rough with him on the playground. Andy was born with birth defects, but he was the sweetest and nicest little guy. Once Jake said to me, "Andy never gets mad. Do you know why?"

"Why?" I was curious.

"Because his parents are never mad at him!"

"Oh, I see." I wanted to meet his little friend's parents.

I picked up the phone and told Julia that Jake would love to go to Andy's birthday party. She sounded so happy, and I made a new friend from that day on.

The birthday party was at an outdoor aquatic park. Julia wore a red cotton dress with purple and pink dots. She had large brown eyes and a constant big smile on her face. Her bangs were hastily clipped to the side with bobby pins as if she didn't have enough time to get her hair styled. It was obvious that Julia had a large circle of friends, and she was busy making sure everyone was comfortable and having a good time.

The minute Julia saw Jake and me, she beamed. "Thank you, thank you so much for coming, Andy will be so happy!"

"This is Linda, Andy's buddy and Jake's mom." She introduced me to all the Asian moms who were sitting by the pool talking amongst themselves or watching the kids playing in the water.

When Andy spotted Jake, he ran to him and forgot about all his other friends who were at the party. They played together for the rest of the afternoon.

Julia's husband John Wang was tall and handsome with a nice haircut and a slick camera in his hand. Joe chatted with him about photography. It turned out that John was self-employed trading used cameras online.

When Andy came to his dad and asked if he and Jake could go to the lazy river, John patted him on the head gently and said he would take them.

Joe and I followed. We waved to them every time their blue tube floated by. John appeared to be a nice guy, soft-spoken, very attentive to Andy and good with kids. They were floating for about half an hour when Julia appeared frenziedly.

"Andy, I have been looking all over for you. It's time to go inside and cut the cake. Hurry up, we need to go!"

"Sorry, Julia! We should have told you before heading this way."

John said nothing and I noticed a sneer on his face. It was subtle but visible. Something was off between Julia and John.

Julia made sure Andy's birthday bash wasn't going to be anything short of a big splash. In the party room, there were dozens of foil birthday balloons tied to each chair. She ordered enough pizza to feed a whole army. Colorful goody bags were placed in a big basket in the middle of the long table. Julia was busy taking care of the details of the party while John took many shots of Andy and his little friends. Throughout the afternoon, Julia and John didn't exchange a single word.

We started spending some time on weekends with Julia and her friends picking vegetables, picnicking at the Forecast Reserve Parks, visiting township fairs. Julia was always alone with Andy. She told us that John had to work on weekends.

One Sunday afternoon as Julia and I were waiting in line with the boys for the hayride, we got into a conversation that validated my suspicion.

"Julia, sorry we couldn't join you yesterday. I was watching my friend's daughter. He and his wife are getting a divorce, and they needed some time alone to work out the details."

Julia's round smiling face fell. "It's good that they can work things out. I've been trying to divorce John for over a year, but he refuses to agree to any of the terms I have proposed. It's been such a pain."

For the first time, I saw pain and anguish beyond that cheerful face. "I am sorry to hear that. I didn't know you were going through a painful divorce, but I have sensed something isn't right between you and John."

"You are one smart lady," She sighed. "John doesn't do anything for Andy. I am the one who takes him to the doctors to discuss with them treatment plans. I am the one who pays the bills and the mortgage. Now I am paying a ton of money to the lawyers. I offered him the lawyer fees in exchange for an amicable divorce, but he wouldn't do it. He doesn't think that I know he rents a fancy apartment and dates other women via online dating services."

"That's, that's unbelievable. In that case why wouldn't he agree to a divorce?"

"He blames me for Andy's birth defects. Somehow he thinks I am in debt to him for the rest of my life. He is determined to squeeze every penny out of me."

It was outrageous that people could be this malicious. Taking care of a child with health issues was already hard enough, and on top of that Julia had to fight this ugly battle with her husband. My heart went out for my new friend.

Julia and I developed a friendship over time. I took Andy home from school whenever she had to be in court. She wanted a divorce so that John could no longer live in her house, and, more importantly, she wanted sole custody of her son. She couldn't take Andy anywhere out of Illinois without John's consent. And most of the time John wouldn't let her know if he was going to sign the required paper until the last minute, even to Wisconsin Dells.

When her parents, who were in their seventies and didn't speak any English visited, John called the cops on them when Julia was at work, complaining of domestic violence. She rushed home trembling behind the wheels and later moved her parents out of the house to spare them of future pain and humiliation. Before every court appearance, Julia hoped it would be the last, but it took much longer than anticipated because John who represented himself kept on calling new witnesses and was determined to drag it out. Julia said John was winning because she was financially drained due to the mounting legal bills. She had wished to have some money left to finance Andy's medical procedures. Andy needed a cardiac pacemaker. Doctors had also recommended a couple of operations to enhance his hearing as Andy only had one ear. I could feel the enormous weight on Julia's shoulder. I wished there was more I could do to help.

\*

Joe and I were on a winding road to rebuild our relationship and home. He was thrilled that someone was finally willing to listen to him with an open-mind and curiosity. He and I had many interesting and thought-provoking discussions about religion, its origin, its social function, the meaning of life outside the realm of religion.

"How do we teach Jake right from wrong without the Biblical guidelines?" I asked Joe the question that had been on my mind.

Joe answered enthusiastically and readily, "A child asks her mother 'Mommy, why can't I lie?' A Christian mother might say 'It displeases God. Lying is sin.' A secular mother's answer could be, 'Because you want to be trusted.' We know right and wrong from our own experiences. The society itself has rules and moral standards in order to maintain its orderliness and stability which is critical to human survival."

"C. S. Lewis claimed that the universal morality or natural law proved there was a God. All people know what this law is and when they break it." I was in the middle of reading *Mere Christianity*.

"Yes, that's his main argument for Christianity. Pastor Dale kind of preached the same point last Sunday: if a little girl is about to be hit by a bus, it'll be viewed as immoral if people just walk by not at all concerned, whether this happens in America, in India, in China, in Africa. They're supposed to do something to save her life. But I watched a video clip recently, you should watch it too. It's very interesting. A bullock was pulled into the water by a crocodile and then a few lions came over and battled the crocodile for the prey. The lions were about to enjoy a satisfying meal when a herd of bull charged towards them, chased them away one by one and restored the bullock to safety. Who inserted this high-standard morality into the bulls and made them willing to sacrifice their own lives to save the weak? It's evolution. Such behavior is important to the survival and continuation of the species."

"That actually makes sense. Now I don't feel that hurt by the rejections we've been receiving from our old circle."

"Tell me why."

"Because from the evolution point of view, the church institute will have to reject anything that threatens its stability and survival. So it's nothing personal," I laughed.

"You're right about that!"

His views towards death tended to be our point of contention.

"If I ever become terminally ill, I may consider taking my own life so that I'll die in dignity without burdening others especially you for too long."

My heart ached. "No, you can't do that! I don't mind taking care of you no matter how hard it gets. I want to be with you for as long as possible. What message are you going to send to our children if you take your own life? That it's OK to give up when things get too tough?"

The Joe I admired so much suddenly became a coward in my eyes. Following a brief silence, Joe opened up. "When my father was in the hospital after the failed surgery to remove the tumors from his lungs, he was in so much pain that he tried more than once to pull the tubes that kept him alive. He wanted to die. I got so mad because in my mind he was the best father in the world who could endure anything and win any battle. I wanted him to fight cancer for my mother and for us." Joe paused for a minute, and then continued, "A few times I purposely slammed the windows on my fingers to keep myself awake at night so that I could keep an eye on my dad."

I didn't know what to say. I wasn't there and so I could only imagine the horrific scene.

"Seeing Rende go through the same pain was harder. There was no quality of life. His wife begged him to eat and forced food on him even though he couldn't hold anything down. She kept on saying the sky was falling."

I tried to imagine what I would have done if I were in my sister-in-law's shoes. Then I thought about a statement Joe had made.

"What did you mean by 'I'd go to heaven after death?'"

"I used to think that heaven was where God was. Now I believe heaven is where one's ego isn't. All religions try to deal with this notion of self. That's why the Bible says 'Whoever wants to be my disciple must deny themselves and take up their cross and follow me.' All our emotional pain and fear of death are originated from the self. When I die, my ego ceases to exist, and therefore I'll be in heaven, a place where there is no pain, no suffering, and no fear."

"But when you die, not just your ego, but your whole being ceases to exist as well."

"That's right."

"I think it is offensive to call yourself a non-believer and yet declare to Christians that you'll go to heaven. To them it's the utmost privilege."

"I didn't say got to their heaven. I said heaven."

"Heaven is heaven. I think you should stop saying that."

"Okay, if that's what you think."

Death wasn't my favorite topic of conversation, but since we were on the subject, I thought I might as well get to the bottom of it. "If you die today, what kind of memorial service do you want, a religious one or not?"

"That'll be up to you. When I die, I'll be gone. But you need to move on. So whatever makes it easier and brings closure for you will be fine with me."

"Please reconsider taking your own life. I hate that idea. It frightens me."

"Okay. I probably should have said that I'd prefer to terminate the use of life sustaining medical treatment or procedures if I were terminally ill and no longer had quality of life."

"When you figure it all out, please make a living will so I'll know what to do in case you can't express your own wishes."

"Thank you, baby! You are the best wife, the best woman in the world!"

\*

It wasn't all smooth sailing now that God was no longer at the top of our marriage triangle. Joe and I argued more and most of the time with regards to how to raise Jake. Joe was in the background when Jane and Michelle grew up, but he had the tendency to blame me when things didn't go right. I resented that even though I blamed myself, too. With Jake, he wanted to be more involved which led to more conflicts. One day my ego took the best of me, and I blew it.

"Jake spends too much time playing computer games. I had to remind him that his time was up all day today," I complained.

"It's not that bad. You're too strict. You expect him to stop immediately every time you tell him to. That's not realistic."

"I let him play because he agreed to stop at a certain time."

"But it's hard to stop in the middle of a game."

"I do give him a five-minute and then a two-minute warning. If I let him go on five more minutes this time, he'll want another ten next time, and it will never end."

"Try to be more flexible. You are too tense sometimes. You make people around you nervous." His criticism sounded particularly harsh that day.

"You keep on downloading these new games for him which isn't helping. And I am not too tense! You're too laid back!"

"Mommy, did you bring my goggles for the pool?" Jake interrupted us from the backseat.

"Yes, I did," I tried to sound normal.

"Oh, good!"

Joe and I entered Lifetime in a sour mood. Jake saw a couple of his friends in the pool and immediately plunged into fun. Less than an hour later, Joe wanted to leave. "It's time to go. I promised Michelle to take her driving this afternoon."

"Jake is having so much fun. I'd rather have him playing outside than sitting in front of a computer at home. Can you pick us up later?" I used the I-am-not-happy-with-you tone of voice.

"Okay." No warmth in his voice either.

I thought Joe and Michelle were going to drive around the neighborhood and could come to us quickly when we were ready to go.

"Jake is ready to go home." I called Joe about an hour later.

"We just got to the lab. It's going to take a while."

So they didn't drive around the neighborhood. Joe took Michelle to the lab where he worked.

"How long do we have to wait?" I had stayed in a long line and bought a strawberry smoothie for Jake, but the lid came off when he took it from my hand, and it splashed. So I got back in line and got another cup. It spilled again the second time. This was a bad day getting worse.

"A couple of hours."

"A couple of hours? You got to be kidding!" I thought he was getting back at me since we had an argument earlier in the car. "Get me a taxi, I want to go home!"

"I don't have the number to call a taxi." He hung up.

"Jakey, Daddy can't come and pick us up right now. How about we walk home?" I tried my best to conceal the boiling anger inside me.

"Why can't he come right now?"

"He is teaching Michelle how to drive."

It was a hot summer day, over 90°F outside. Jake and I started our long journey home on foot. I held his little hand while carrying his beach bag, my workout bag, and my purse on my shoulder.

I called Joe again. "Since you can't pick us up, Jake and I are walking home. Bye!" I hung up.

My cell phone kept on ringing. I ignored it and eventually turned it off.

Walking seemed to calm me. I felt sorry for dragging Jake into this.

"Jakey, Mommy isn't mad at you for playing too many computer games. But we need to work out some rules so that both you and I can enjoy what we like to do. I actually don't enjoy nagging you all day."

"Okay, Mommy. And I am sorry for spilling the drinks at the pool."

"It's not your fault. Accidents happen. It's OK."

Jake grinned.

Sweat was dripping from Jake's hair and face after walking for about a mile. We stopped at Dairy Queen and ordered two cold drinks. The air condition felt really good.

"Mommy, I am ready to go." Jake stood up and moved towards the door.

I was surprised he asked to leave so quickly. The poor little fellow wanted to be home.

The next mile was harder. Jake didn't like his lemonade chiller. So we stopped at Wendy's to get him a Sprite. This time we sat inside a little longer. Joe found us a few feet away from Wendy's. I buckled Jake in his car seat, dumped the bags on the backseat, and kept on going. I was determined to walk the remaining four miles and get home on my own.

I started working out at Lifetime regularly a year ago. The running, lifting and sweating had been doing amazing things for me. I found myself in a happy mood after a good workout. The book *The Science of Happiness* by Stefan Klein provided scientific reasons for this phenomenon. Happiness is linked to one's body. When one feels good, her blood circulation improves, skin temperature rises ever so slightly and shoulder and neck muscles relax. The body sends the messages to the brain that in turn releases serotonin that puts her in an uplifting and positive mood. On the other hand, a lower level of serotonin may influence mood in a way that leads to depression. With the backing of the scientific evidence and personal experience, I continued to go to the gym and exercise religiously. My neck and back pain went away, my mood, body, and sleeping patterns all improved. During our last family vacation, I put on a bikini for the first time in my life, thoroughly enjoying myself in the sun on the heaven-like Cancun beach.

The sky was getting dark and a few raindrops landed on my forehead. At the corner of my eye, I caught a glimpse of Joe's white Lexus whizzing by. He honked and turned the right blinker on indicating he was going to wait for me at the next corner ahead. I stuck out my middle finger and continued walking. I didn't need a ride from him.

The combination of the long walk, the sweat, and the aromatic smell of the grass ahead of a storm did its magic for me. I was able to think logically and sensibly. This ego thing could be hard to manage when not restrained by the fear of God. It was absolutely wrong to drag Jake into this fight. Joe and I would have to find a new way to settle our differences and maintain a harmonious relationship.

The rain held out until I got home after the three-hour journey on foot, and I was no longer mad. As a matter of fact, I had a new goal in mind, which was to find a way to remain humble, flexible, and compassionate in the wake of the deepened self-understanding and a newfound voice with increasing clarity. Joe and the kids already had dinner. So I ate and cleaned up the kitchen.

At night, Joe, being the nice and rational guy, apologized. "I am sorry about today. I was stuck between you and Michelle, the two demanding women in my life. She wanted to practice more at the lab so that she would pass the road test."

"I blew it. I am sorry. I thought you were giving me a hard time because of our disagreement."

"You know it wasn't safe to walk with Jake like that."

"You are absolutely right and we shouldn't have argued in front of Jake. Maybe we need to set up some rules so that things don't get out of hand in the future."

"Like a fighting protocol. I like it. Do you mind drafting it?"

The next day I emailed Joe the following protocol:

1. We will discuss child-rearing issues with an open mind not during crisis, but when things are calm.
2. We will not criticize each other's parenting skills in front of our children.
3. Joe will be sensitive to Linda's menstrual cycles. Linda will not challenge Joe when he is upset.
4. Joe will take the initiative for reconciliation after an argument or fight (as he always does). Linda will try her best to accept his warm gesture immediately.
5. Linda welcomes Joe's effort on trying to get more involved with Jake's life. Joe will try to introduce other interesting things to Jake besides computer and games.
6. We will earn each other's respect instead of locking into the mentality that one has to follow the lead of the other.

Joe thought it was a good start, and we both agreed that it would change along with time and circumstances. For a while things chugged along without glitches. But like any rules made with good intention, if the people who were supposed to follow them repeatedly failed to do so, after a while they simply ceased to exist.

\*

Not all Asian mothers are tiger moms, although I desired for my children to achieve academic excellence and make an admirable living. My aspiration reflected typical Chinese value: the pursuit of education and a promising career. In Mainland China due to the one-child policy introduced in 1978, this aspiration had become an obsession. Parents took their babies who weren't even walking to English classes. Once kids entered elementary school, they were loaded with homework and tutoring classes and barely had any time to play.

Influenced by the Western pursuit of freedom and self-fulfillment, Joe and I tried hard to strike a balance between the two cultures, but it wasn't always easy. I used to spend half an hour with Jane and another half an hour with Michelle practicing piano five days a week since Jane was six and Michelle was four. There was yelling and crying occasionally, but I wouldn't let them quit. They were also sent to Chinese School for a couple of hours every Saturday afternoon. The school adopted the traditional Chinese teaching methodology: memorizing, homework, and weekly testing as well as mid-term and final exams. I helped them with their homework and test preparations. The girls weren't having fun, and they couldn't understand why they had to learn Chinese that was so difficult and boring. To me, it was not optional because of their heritage. On weekdays, they were not allowed to watch TV or have Internet access after ten o'clock in the evening. Surprisingly, the rules were held in place until Jane entered her senior year in high school.

To get them rooted in God's word, I read the Bible and prayed with them daily. We also acted out some of the famous Bible stories. Following the example of a Christian home schooling family of eight children, I modeled their mother's obedience training practice. I would ask Jane and Michelle to go upstairs and play in their room and come to the kitchen immediately when they were called.

"Michelle, come to the kitchen please." I would call with music in my voice as Mrs. Martin did with her delightful children.

"Coming, Mommy!" Michelle's little feet ran happily and hastily down the staircase.

"Jane, come to the kitchen, please."

"Okay, coming!"

We would practice over and over again until they really got it.

Mrs. Martin came to Peter's Fellowship a few times to share her child rearing experience. Her eight children were all well behaved and self-motivated. Her view that delayed obedience was disobedience struck a chord with me. I'd become exhausted from having to constantly remind the girls of what they were supposed to do. This not only provided the biblical validation but also the means to obtain immediate obedience from my children. As the training went on, I was less inclined to comprise and negotiate.

Jane was a smart, cute, and super-active little girl with bright sparkling eyes, long silky black hair, and a naughty grin. She jumped around swiftly and skillfully like Tom the Cat in "Tom and Jerry." I got pregnant with Michelle right after Jane's first birthday. I loved taking naps with Jane on weekends with Michelle in my tummy. Jane enjoyed touching my bulging belly and feeling Michelle kicking and moving inside me. I told her she was going to be a big sister. She was so proud!

For a couple of years, my grandmother took care of Jane when Joe and I were at work. Jane could pretty much get whatever she wanted by screaming and crying and her great grandma would give in eventually. She was one of those kids who would throw a tantrum in the store if we told her she couldn't get something. She also had to try everything out and learn it the hard way. When she was three and Michelle was one, she cut Michelle's hair and hid it behind the toy chest in the toy room, but she couldn't hide Michelle. Joe and I gasped when we saw Michelle's new hairdo that revealed her scalp at a few spots. Michelle had to have her whole head shaved, and she looked like a boy for a few months.

We placed Jane at a daycare right after Michelle was born. She had a very hard time adjusting because we didn't set clear boundary for her at home and also because spending most of her time home with her great grandma meant she didn't speak much English. On her first day, she tried to cut the line to get on the slide. Her teacher lovingly but consistently brought back to the end of the line. Jane screamed and cried each time.

Although they fought constantly and Jane and Michelle could have had their separate rooms, they chose to share the same bedroom until Michelle was almost eight. I used to buy two sets of everything hoping to eliminate the reason for sibling bickering, but it never worked. For some strange reason they were able to notice the slightest differences and decided that one was better than the other. Jane liked to take things apart and Michelle wanted to keep her stuff in perfect condition. When Jane broke her stuff and tried to make a trade with Michelle, a storm was imminent.

"Michelle, do you want to trade your piggy beanie baby with mine? Please?" Jane begged.

"No! You cut the tag off yours. Mommy told us not to cut it off."

"Pleeeease, Michelle. If you let me have yours, you can have my new eraser."

"I don't want your eraser anymore."

"How about I'll also give you my white tank top? Remember yours has a stain on it."

"No! You can't have my piggy!"

Jane grabbed the beanie baby from Michelle's hands. Michelle came to me crying.

"Mommy, I told Jane I didn't want to trade my piggy, but she grabbed it from me anyway!"

"Jane! How many times do I have to tell you to use words only? You got the first pick. Piggy is brand new. Why do you want to trade?" I walked from the kitchen to the family room with Michelle in tow.

"I cut the tags off, but accidentally cut too much." Jane was in tears. I picked up the injured piggy from the floor. "I told you to leave the tags on. Why don't you listen?"

"I don't want the tags. Can you buy me another one, Mommy?"

"No, I can't buy you another one. You ruined your piggy. You'll have to live with it, and don't force Michelle to trade things with you. You're the big sister, and we expect you to take care of Michelle. But instead you make her mad all the time!"

"You only like Michelle! You don't love me!" she wailed and ran upstairs to her room.

"Yes, I love you too! But I don't like how you behave sometimes!" I shouted after her.

BAM! She slammed her door shut.

"What's going on?" Joe peered in in the midst of all the commotions.

"Jane damaged her beanie baby and wanted Michelle's," I sighed.

"Stop buying them so many beanie babies. There are bags of these things in the basement. You're wasting money, plus they always end up fighting."

"Stop buying toys won't stop their fights. They argue over everything, even a piece of paper. You know that. We have to teach Jane to change her forceful ways. She needs to act like a big sister."

"They have way too many toys, and it isn't good for them," Joe insisted before retreating to the study room.

Jane's teen years were turbulent. In her junior year, Jane pretty much gave up on keeping up with the grades and instead devoted all her time to the worship team at Living Water Church and hanging out with friends.

"Jane, this is the most important year of high school. You need to think about college, your GPA and ACTs." Joe and I tried to remind her constantly. We desperately wanted her to get into a good college.

"I know! You don't have to tell me all the time."

"But you're not spending enough time on schoolwork!"

"It's not like I am out there doing drugs or having sex like some of my classmates are doing. I am always at church and hanging out with friends from church!"

"Serving God is good. But don't use that as an excuse. It honors God when you do well academically."

"Asian parents! All you care about is school, grades, and college." She rolled her eyes and walked away.

In spite of our repeated insistence, Jane wouldn't come home before curfew after her Friday night fellowship at Living Water. I couldn't fall asleep until I knew she was home safe. And so I started texting and calling her after 10:30.

"Why are you always calling me? I don't know when I'm coming home. My friends and I are going to McDonald's." She bellowed.

"You shouldn't be out there so late according to the curfew law."

"No other parents are looking for their kids. Why can't you just go to sleep?"

"I can't sleep until I know you're home safe! You'll understand that someday when you become a mother yourself."

"Go to sleep. Don't wait for me." She hung up.

Even though family was the most important thing to me, my focus had always been external. I believed that if I loved and served God with all my heart, everything else would fall into place. So when some kind-hearted sisters called and informed me Jane had misbehaved in church or had worn something inappropriate, it disturbed me greatly. I felt I had failed as a mother, the most important job of my life. I'd pour my frustration on Jane, trying to make her see things the way I did and when all failed I prayed she would behave appropriately not for me but for God.

One Friday night, she was still out after midnight. Joe picked up the phone and issued an ultimatum. "Jane, if you are not home in ten minutes, your car won't be running tomorrow when you need to go out. I'll make sure of that!"

She got home in less than ten minutes.

Even though I no longer attended service at Living Water, I felt the need to email the youth director and the English deacon asking them to end the evening program at a reasonable time and guide our adolescents to be law-abiding citizens by going home before curfew. We were worried about Jane, not sure if she would be able to get into a decent college or make wise choices after leaving home. But I knew I had to change and let go of the traditional ways of relating to her, otherwise she and I would continue to be stuck in our relationship. I couldn't risk losing a precious daughter who was about to fly on her own.

When she dressed appropriately for church, I complimented her. When she started working on her homework right after coming home from work on a weekday, I made her a snack and commented lovingly, "It must be a long day for you. Don't stay up too late, OK?"

She took my advice and studied for ACT a couple of weeks before her third try.

"Mom, Mom!" she sounded frantic on the phone, almost like she was crying.

"What's the matter? Are you in a car accident? Are you hurt?" My heart pounded uncontrollably.

"Calm down mother. I am OK. Guess what?"

"What?"

"I got a thirty-three on my ACT!"

I took a deep sigh of relief. "That's so great! I'm so proud of you! I knew you could do it if you just put your mind to it." She improved seven points from her last test.

"Thank you! Yes, I did it. I am very happy!" she laughed proudly.

For a couple of years when she was between fourteen and fifteen, Jane cringed every time I touched her like I had a disease. After Jake was born, we developed the tradition of dressing up for Christmas pictures with Joe serving as our family photographer. I looked constrained in the pictures with Jane and Michelle. We each stood in our own space without physical contact. In the course of a few years, the three of us got more lively, intimate, and creative posing for the camera. The gaps among us shrunk in front of the camera and in real life.

*I am going to share a close relationship with my girls, contrary to what I have with my mother. Even though I've never felt this way before, I am sad for my mother for what she has missed in life. I wish I could, but I just can't love her as a mother because she has never been one to me.*

When Jane was directly admitted to the Kelley School of Business at Indiana University with a partial scholarship, Joe and I were thrilled.

Living Water Church hosted a senior banquet to send the kids off to college. The gym in the basement was decorated with balloons, colorful streamers, and banners. Each graduate went up to the microphone and expressed his or her gratitude to the family, church, and friends. Some kids had their speech all written out, some appeared spontaneous, and some were eloquent. Jane being Jane, made a few notes in her cell phone last minute, got up there, and babbled. I had to admit she looked beautiful in a pink one-shoulder chiffon cocktail dress with two pink flowers on the strap. Her long black hair youthfully cascaded down her back. Even though she kept glancing at her phone and was busy with her hand gesture, she looked more confident and at ease with herself than ever.

*In spite of all the growing pains, my little girl is turning into a beautiful woman!* I choked up at the thought.

My biggest wish was for Jane to stay safe while flying high and remember to fly home every once in a while. I was secretly afraid that her new life would be so exciting that she would forget us altogether. Occasionally I still received phone calls reporting Jane's mischief. I would calmly tell Jane what I heard and let her decide if she wanted to adjust her behavior or appearance.

Just when I believed we had turned the corner, things went downhill a short while before Jane was to leave for college. On a hot summer morning, I got a call from her best friend Connie's mom. "Linda, the girls want to go the Indiana Dunes. They asked Connie to drive. But her car is really old and not safe. We don't feel comfortable about it. Peter is working from home today. He offered to drive them, but the girls don't want him."

I called Jane who was at Connie's house. "Jane, Connie's mom doesn't think her car is safe. So please don't go today."

"It's OK, mom. Nothing is going to happen to the car. We'll be careful." I could barely hear her with all the other girls talking and laughing at the same time.

"Just don't go. Safety first, OK?" I warned her.

She called me an hour later from Connie's car, already on the road to the Dunes. I was livid.

Her reckless behavior again caused us to question her judgment. Joe and I tried to talk to her the next day.

"Why are you making such a big deal out of it? We got home safe, right?" Her tone was very disrespectful.

"What if something did happen? What if the car broke down on the highway?" Joe was visibly upset.

"Nothing happened. I don't want to talk about it anymore. I'm eighteen. I don't need anyone to tell me what to do."

Joe lost it. "If you think you are all grown up and don't need our help and advice anymore, leave and try to make it on your own and see what happens."

Jane stood up and left the dinner table.

An hour later, I was reading to Jake in his room. Michelle came in. "Jane packed all her stuff and left." I was gripped by a wave of panic.

After getting Jake settled for bed, I tried to get hold of Jane, but she wouldn't pick up her phone. Joe called Sprint and instructed them to cut all service on Jane's phone with the exception of allowing her to receive calls. I was worried to death.

"Go to sleep. Let her be," Joe grunted. He fell asleep quickly like he always did.

I couldn't fall asleep without knowing where Jane was and whether she was OK.

Jane finally called before midnight. "My phone doesn't work anymore. What did Dad do?"

"He terminated the service. You can only receive calls."

"Why did he do that?"

"Because you wouldn't take our calls. So you aren't coming home? I noticed you withdrew all the money in your checking account."

"I was afraid you were going to take my money. I'm spending the night at Leslie's. I am coming home tomorrow."

"It would have been nice if you had told us before you left."

"But Dad kicked me out of the house." She started crying.

"He was just mad. Put yourself in our shoes."

"Can you ask him to restore the service?"

"You'll have to talk to him yourself when you come home tomorrow."

Joe and Jane mended things sort of. She still believed that we had overreacted. Joe thought his reaction was justified. Neither father nor daughter formally apologized. Joe got his point across that he did what he did out of deep love and concern.

The day for Jane to move to college finally came. Mentally I was ready to let her go, and she appeared very ready to leave home. She and I hugged and hugged again. Joe was calmer and more composed.

"Jane, be prudent and make wise decisions, OK?" Joe repeated the same line several times.

"Okay, Dad!"

Seeing her empty room every time I went upstairs to collect laundry was weird. A week after Jane left, I texted her after meeting with Lin and Charlotte in the basement to say good night as we had been doing every day. I couldn't fall asleep after our little dialogue. Much to my surprise, Jane was lonely and very homesick, but it made me happy to know she missed us and still needed us. I was hopeful and positive she and I would connect more deeply in spite of the distance separating us.

Jane and I communicated daily. She told me the major events in her life, what she missed the most of living at home, and her plans for the near future. I was glancing at my cell phone almost every minute when she was waiting for a phone call from the Alpha Kappa Psi's leader. Her last interview didn't go as well as she'd expected as expressed by her text messages.

Late that evening, I got a text from her: "I got accepted to AKPsi!!!!!!!!" I picked up the phone immediately. "So proud of you! All your hard work paid off! You can't imagine how thrilled I am!" She was elated!

Our Jane started to shine in college. She was devoted to AKPsi while keeping up with class assignments. Her friends voted her the chaplain of the fraternity at the end of freshman year, and her grades made her Asian parents very proud. Our baby was finally working hard and building a bright future for herself.

Jane didn't have any serious relationships in high school. We watched her agonizing over a boy who went from one girl to the next. Eventually she came to the realization that it wasn't worth it. So when the boy finally asked her to be his girlfriend, she said no. When she came home from college for the first winter break, I asked her casually "Anything new in your life? Any boys I need to know about?"

"Yes! Actually I like this boy ..." She pulled a chair next to mine in the kitchen.

I knew this was serious. "What's his name? How old is he?" I realized I sounded like a typical Asian mom.

"His name is Jim, and he is white. He's a sophomore, a year older than me."

"How long have you known each other?"

"We met in AKpsi. We've known each other since the beginning of the semester. He told me recently that he liked me."

"What did you say?"

"I told him I wasn't ready for any serious relationships yet and so let's just be cool about it."

I was impressed by my girl's response.

"Do you want to see a picture of him?" Jane grinned.

"Sure!" Jane showed me a picture of her with Jim from her iPhone. Jane looked smitten in it. Jim was more than a head taller than Jane and very good-looking with a genuine big smile. I knew my daughter's different and sometimes exaggerated facial expressions, but this was a happy and content from the bottom of her heart glow.

A couple of months later, Jane announced on her Facebook that she was in relationship with Jim.

Jim hit a homerun with us, Joe especially, when he asked to meet us at the end of the school year. The two families ended up having lunch together as we were on campus the same day to move our kids back home.

\*

If Jane sometimes made me feel inadequate, Michelle brought assurance to my motherhood. She is as pretty as Jane, taller, with large brown eyes that can talk, and a very pleasing smile. Since the girls are less than two years apart, I used to dress them in identical clothes, and people thought they were twins.

Michelle room was always neat with things in their proper places. She was willing to work hard to reach for that "A" instead of settling for a B." Michelle asked for permission to do something instead of telling us about it after the fact. People told me that Michelle took her look after me and Jane from Joe. In her room on the nightstand, there was a picture of her dressed in a pink gown gracefully looking down. I definitely saw a glimpse of me in that picture.

As a little girl, Michelle had the charisma of a princess and looked upon everyone else as means to serve her needs. Her preschool teacher told me Michelle had all the boys in class running around getting things for her. They did it happily and willingly. "Michelle, what do you want to be when you grow up?" I asked her when she was three. "I want to be rr-rich!" she replied proudly.

For her twelfth birthday, Michelle wanted to invite about a dozen friends. Since some of them didn't get along, she asked me to host two parties so that half of her friends could come to one and the other half to the other. I could see myself doing something like this to make every guest happy, so I went along with it. Joe thought it was ridiculous. Michelle had me running around twice as hard so that she could enjoy a perfect birthday celebration. She and Joe were sometimes at odds because of her tendency to complicate things and make not so sensible requests according to Joe's standard.

Michelle threatened to leave home at the age of five when she was very upset. "I'm going to the woods." She put on her backpack and stood by the door with fat tears trickling down her cheeks.

"Who is going to take care of you in the woods?" I asked.

"I don't care. I am going, and nobody can stop me!"

"Michelle, you are right we can't stop you. But I have to tell you that there are bears in the woods and they'd love to gobble up little girls like you for dinner." Joe took up an exaggerated spooky tone.

Michelle was still glued to the door, her mind churning. After a few minutes, she turned around. "I don't feel like going today, maybe tomorrow."

"Good choice, Michelle. Can Daddy go with you tomorrow?"

"Maybe." She tried hard not to smile.

We took Jane and Michelle to China a few times usually during the summer break. Michelle didn't like the hot sticky summer in Shanghai.

"I'm too hot and tired. I want to go back to the apartment," she complained the minute we stepped out of the apartment building.

"But did you say you wanted to go to the store and buy some pencils and note pads?"

"I just want to go back. Can we go back, please?"

We turned around without even venturing into the street. She stayed in the air-conditioned room with the remote control in her hand making sure the temperature was exactly at 27°C.

In high school, Michelle had to work hard every summer to make the cut for the tennis team. She would play for hours in the heat. When we advised her to skip a day due to the dangerously high temperature. She chose to go anyway with a big jug of water in her hand.

"Oh, my God! It was so hot! I couldn't breathe. I almost died!" Michelle complained loudly when she came back.

"I told you not to go." Joe smiled at her fondly.

She turned golden brown after a few weeks. People thought she was Hawaiian or Mexican. She looked stunning with her tanned and toned figure.

When Michelle was fifteen, Joe and I went to China with Jake for a couple of weeks in October. Michelle sounded really excited one day when I called her from China.

"Mom, mom, I want to tell you something."

"What is it?"

"I have a boyfriend!"

I couldn't believe I had only been gone for less than a week and she already had a boyfriend. I wasn't sure how to react, but I knew I shouldn't overreact.

"Who is this boy? Is he somebody I know?"

"You don't know him. He's from school. His mom is Chinese and his dad American. He's the champion cross-country runner in our school."

"What's his name?"

"Tim. His name is Tim."

"I'd love to meet Tim when I get back."

"Okay!"

"Michelle, don't do anything. Don't have—you know you are too young for that."

"What are you talking about mom? I won't do anything like that."

"Good!"

Part of me was excited since Michelle was at the same age as I was when I fell in love with Joe. She could have found the love of her life young as well.

"Oh, Mom, I'm only fifteen. I may not even get married." Michelle tried to contain my excitement.

"Of course you're going to get married. There is no if about it!"

"Sure, woman, if that's what you think," she said jokingly.

Six weeks later Michelle informed us that she had broken up with Tim.

"What happened?"

"Well, it's too much work having a boyfriend. I'm not going to marry him anyway. So what's the point?"

I was relieved and disappointed at the same time.

Learning from past headaches, I asked Michelle to sign a contract before agreeing to take her for her driving test. She signed and kept her word for the most part. I was a lot more relaxed the second time around which sure helped things quite a bit.

"Mom, do you know the farthest place Michelle has driven to is the Fox Valley Mall and she still has to use her GPS to get there?" Jane told me one day after Michelle had been driving for six months.

I laughed. Michelle definitely had my genes. I got mine from my mother. When my parents were dating, my father would consult my mother if he was confused with which way to go. He usually picked the opposite direction my mother suggested, and it always worked. I couldn't get anywhere without the GPS, the best gift Joe had ever given to me. I teased Joe by saying that my GPS was my second husband.

I urged Michelle to work hard and get an equal or better score on ACT than Jane. With her higher GPA, I was sure she could get into an even better college. Michelle pushed back.

"Mom, I have a lot of homework and other things going on in my life. I don't have time to study for ACT right now."

"I know you are very busy. But study whenever you have time, OK?"

"O-K, woman! I know what I am doing." She was annoyed.

I felt I had to give her one last lecture before giving up nagging. "I know you have a lot going on, but you know college is important for your future. I'll stop nagging because I can tell you're annoyed with me. It's your future, and it's up to you what you want to make out of it. Well, the truth is you've been a wonderful girl and always seem to know what the right thing is to do. So I am just going to trust that you'll continue to do that. I'll stop bothering you, I promise."

"Okay, Mom. I'll do my best," she assured me.

In her junior year, she got a job at a newly opened frozen yogurt store. I wished she would spend more time studying in the most critical year of high school instead of working, but I knew she was happy. Barely lifting a finger at home, at work Michelle served customers, wiped tables, took out the garbage to the dumpster, and cleaned the bathrooms. Our little princess was getting a dosage of reality, and it was a good thing.

Even though both Jane and Michelle practically grew up in church, Michelle stopped going to Living Water not too long after we left. She told me that kids were talking loudly or texting when the sermon was preached. So she didn't get much out of it anymore. And for some reason, she and her church friends had grown apart. Meanwhile, she was bonding with a few girls from school. I didn't try to influence her one way or the other. I knew her friends from school were hardworking, honest, and from solid families. I wasn't worried about Michelle.

A few of my old friends expressed serious concern over Michelle's separation from the church, the same concern when an alcoholic quit going to AA meetings. To them, we, particularly teens, were all sinners and needed to have fellowship with each other in the body of Christ to strengthen our faith and keep us on the right course. Some parents viewed church and God as insurance to their kids' wellbeing. I now believed that a strong family tie, solid friends, and self-motivation were critical to their continued success.

After years of never-ending bickering, Jane and Michelle had become each other's best friend. Whenever Jane came home from college, the girls were inseparable. They talked, giggled, laughed and talked more. If Michelle had boy issues or questions about colleges, they'd arrange online face time to have a lengthy discussion.

*

Jake is a handsome boy with large smiling brown eyes, long eyelashes and an adorable smile that melts your heart. When he laughs, it sounds like a string of pearls break loose and bounces on the tile floor. Jake was an effective communicator right out of the gate. He gave us clear signals when he was hungry, wet, or needed to go to bed. I learned to listen to him instead of assuming I knew what the best for him was.

Jake's growing assertiveness was both gratifying and risky. Both Jane and Michelle were shy when they were little, but Jake would strike a conversation with anyone at the grocery store, in the library, or park. We loved his self-confidence and fabulous verbal ability. But the flipside was one never knew what would come out of his mouth especially when he wasn't happy.

"Stop telling me what to do, Daddy! I only listen to my coach. You are annoying me." Jake stomped to the sideline and gave Joe such an angry stare.

After a moment of awkward silence, Joe resumed his easy-going demeanor. "Okay, Jake. Daddy was only trying to help. You do whatever you need to do out there, I'll stop telling you what to do."

One time when Jake was not even three, he and I went grocery shopping. In the produce department, there was a puddle of milk on the floor.

"Look at this mess!" I pointed for Jake to see.

"Who did it?"

"I don't know. But somebody surely made a big mess here."

What he said next was both surprising and thought provoking. "Well, accidents do happen, and it's OK."

"You are right, baby. It's OK." I occasionally overreacted when he spilled milk or juice on the wooden kitchen floor.

Another time at daycare he told a new teacher who he hadn't seen before, "This is my class. I don't know you. I want you to leave." His class teacher Ms. Rhonda was very surprised because Jake was normally a pleasant and polite boy.

Ms. Rhona told me very proudly how Jake stood up for himself when another kid hit him several times. "Please don't hit me. I don't like it when you hit me. I'll appreciate it if you stop hitting me. Thank you!" He wasn't even four years old at the time.

When Jake was four, Joe and I took him to the doctor's office for regular checkup and shots. I didn't tell him he was going to get shots in order not to prolong his misery. His mood deteriorated in the waiting room. He asked again and again if he was getting shots, and I told him we'd find out when we saw the doctor. When Dr. Wey came into the room with the needle in her hand, Jake fought with all his might. It took four people, the doctor, her assistant, Joe, and me to hold him down.

He screamed at Dr. Wey who was a very small Asian woman not much bigger than Jake, "I don't like you! You are not my friend! I don't want to see you again! I hope you'll be out of the job, so you can't give shots anymore!" All of us tried not to laugh. He got sweaty from kicking and crying, and his forehead was covered with little red dots when it was all done.

I asked him in the car, "Jake, was all that kicking and screaming necessary? The shot took five seconds, but you made it much harder than it needed to be."

"I just don't like shots." He took a deep sigh and continued sucking on his lollipop.

"Did it hurt that bad?"

"Not really."

"So can we try to be a little calmer next time?"

"Sure!" he sounded so enthusiastic his voice squeaked.

Jake tripped in his classroom a few days before Christmas and had a long and deep cut slightly above the right side of his upper lip. He had calmed down in his teacher's arms when I got there. His lip was swollen although the bleeding of his gum had stopped.

"What should I do? Should I take him the doctor or directly to emergency?" I mumbled to myself.

All the staff members surrounding Jake all smiled at me empathetically without offering an opinion one way or the other.

"You know what, Jake? We'll call Daddy and he'll know what to do."

Joe thought I should take him to Dr. Wey first. She advised us to go to the ER because Jake would need a few stitches. Joe met us at the Hinsdale emergency room.

"Jakey, let Daddy take a look." Joe slowly peeled the bandage and looked closely at the ugly cut, his nose almost touching Jake's face, his eyebrows turned into a knot. "Oh, poor little thing! It must hurt a lot. We'll have to get this fixed so that it won't leave a scar on your face."

Jake nodded.

"Listen to Daddy, Jakey. You're going to need stitches. It'll hurt a little." Joe tried to prep Jake for what was coming.

"What's stitches, Daddy?"

"Well, they are going to sew up the cut on top of your lip just like when Daddy used a needle and thread to fix your little blanket."

"Is it going to hurt a lot?"

"They'll use medicine so it won't hurt that much. But Daddy needs you to be very brave. Everyone in this hospital is your friend. They want to help you and make you feel better. Do you understand?"

"I know, Dad."

When the doctor and nurse showed up in our little emergency room, Jake was his talkative and happy self. The doctor was a middle-aged, medium-built man who had dark skin and a cheerful demeanor and appeared experienced with treating children. The nurse was young, tall, and stout with a baby face and big grin. His job was to hold Jake's head during the procedure. The nurse gave Jake a little toy car, which made him even happier. They wrapped and bound Jake's body in this thick blue plastic thing to restrain him from moving. With his head firmly cupped in the nurse's big hands, Jake looked nervous and scared. I noticed bean-sized sweat oozing from his forehead, but he remained motionless.

The small room was getting uncomfortably crowded, and I couldn't bear to see what was going to happen next. So I excused myself and paced in the hallway, paying attention to any sound coming from the room. I heard Joe talking to Jake the whole time. "Jake, you are such a brave boy! It'll be done soon. Daddy's right here with you." Jake was quiet.

Fifteen minutes later, the door opened, and out came the nurse still grinning.

"He is the bravest four-year-old I have ever seen!"

I hurried into the room. "Jakey, Mommy's so proud of you. You stayed still and didn't even make a sound!"

A big smile spread across Jake's face. He was so proud of himself!

"He's an amazing boy. You guys did a great job too." The doctor smiled at us while releasing Jake from the wrap. "Some parents are more hysterical than their kids, which makes our job trickier."

Jake didn't connect with our families in China the same way Jane and Michelle did. He found it annoying when all of them wanted to touch him and hold him. Jake entered daycare at the age of two and had forgotten all of his Chinese by the time he was three. He spoke to the folks in Shanghai in English and assumed they understand him because they always responded with "yes" and "okay." One day it dawned on him that nobody really knew what he was saying when he asked my mother and a few others for juice and they just kept on smiling and nodding without ever bringing him the juice.

"These people aren't very smart. They don't even know what 'juice' means," Jake concluded indignantly.

"They speak Chinese. They might think you aren't very smart since you don't speak their language."

Jake asked me to teach him Chinese when we got back to Chicago, and I taught him a new word each day.

Jake was receptive to advice given in a loving and caring tone. Once he was convinced that it was good to do something, he would do it consistently. Jake believed it was irresponsible to waste electricity, so he always turned off the lights in an empty room in our house. For a few years, he went to bed at exactly 8:22 pm. I couldn't remember why it was 8:22 and not 8:30, but he and I agreed it was a good time for bed. He would be playing in his room and when the digital clock showed 8:22 in large red numbers, he would quickly stop what he was doing and settle into bed.

Jake spent the first four years of his life playing and exploring. Every day he and I enjoyed an hour together before bedtime reading, playing, and cuddling. It was our sacred time. I was in no hurry to rush him into anything. I had realized from raising Jane and Michelle that I could make them learn things and get fairly good at them, but I couldn't make them love anything. Michelle quit piano when she joined the tennis team in high school. She barely touched piano again after that even though she had won many prizes in competitions. Both girls came to me after Jake was born expressing their desire to quit Chinese school. I was seriously overloaded at the time and, out of my character, granted their wish. But they both chose Chinese in high school. Jane took it in college as well.

"Mommy, sign me up for the tennis class. Grant is in it, and he said it was a lot of fun," Jake instructed me when he was close to five.

I signed him up after he had brought it up at least three times.

After a couple of sessions, he didn't think tennis was that much fun anymore. I managed to get to his daycare a few minutes earlier on Thursdays before his lesson.

"Jake, let's go. You have tennis today."

"Mommy, I don't want to go. Can we skip it today?"

"I'll get you a snack when we're there. Remember the goodies in the vending machine?"

"Yeah!"

I let him choose a snack every time, and he stopped saying he didn't want to go. Actually he always told me he had fun after the class. Positive association worked!

We had been using the point system presented by Dr. Alan E. Kazdin in his book *The Kazdin Method for Parenting the Defiant Child* to develop the desirable behavior in Jake. It worked like a charm. The method didn't sound revolutionary, but the devil was in the details. Instead of punishing unwanted behavior, Dr. Kazdin suggests that parents define the positive opposite of that unwanted behavior for their children. By praising enthusiastically whenever the positive opposite occurs and rewarding them with points consistently, the children are likely to demonstrate the desirable behavior regularly and within a short period of time without the points. Jake was rewarded with Lego toys with the points he earned. He would go online to research to choose his next prize. Then we would agree on the number of points needed to get it.

"Mom, the Power Ranger Samurai Megazord I really want costs $27.99 online and $40 in the store. So we should buy online, right?"

"Right. You'll need seventy points for that. If you go to bed at 9:30 without me reminding you, you get five points. And if you do it everyday, it only takes two weeks to get the Samurai Megazord."

"Got it, Mom!" His thumb went up.

Jake wasn't interested in the little rewards along the way to keep him going, he simply aimed at the big prize at the end. Being a creative child, he created multiple opportunities to earn extra points.

"Mommy, I just made my bed. Can you give me two points?" he would ask enthusiastically.

"Mom, how about this: if I go to bed before 9:30, you give me three extra points."

"Jake, I love to give you more points. But I need to save money to buy the toy. If you get enough points today, you'll still have to wait since I don't have enough money yet."

"Do you have $27.99 today?"

"No, not yet."

"Oh, OK."

With Dr. Kazdin's method based on science and decades of cumulative research, we had trained Jake to stay at the table until he finished his meals, to turn off the lights and go to bed, and to have a good attitude towards homework. I didn't forbid Jake from playing computer games or watching TV as I did with Jane and Michelle. As a matter of fact I tried to say "yes" to him every time he asked, but he had to stop at the agreed time, whether it was five, ten, or fifteen minutes later.

"Mommy, mommy, I have to go to the bathroom. That doesn't count as my time on the computer, OK?" Jake shouted as he was running to the bathroom.

"OK. Take your time," I laughed.

Building a more flexible, trusting, and loving relationship with each of my children was far more enjoyable and healthy than the rigid, confrontational, and patriarchal one I grew up in. I was deeply satisfied from within although my relationship with Joe was choppy and in need of a transformation.

*

"I've found out who Mr. Copycat is." Joe came into the kitchen from the garage with a big announcement. I was getting dinner ready.

"Who?" It had been the million-dollar question for the past seven years.

"It's our friend Ryan from Living Water."

"Ryan the Righteous? You got to be kidding." In my mind, I knew he wasn't kidding. "How did you find out?"

"One of my vendors asked me today if I carried lamination machines. I said no. But he told me Ryan Gao carried them and also sold paper cutters just like mine."

"Wow! Unthinkable! All those years I sat and prayed with him in the same BOD meetings while he was backstabbing us. It's unreal!"

"I know! Remember we had dinner with him and his wife last Christmas for Peter's birthday? He kept on teasing Peter and me as the big bosses with deep pockets, while he was only making a living on a meager salary? He is so fake!"

Joe found out later via an Internet search that there were two companies recently registered under Ryan's and his wife's names in Illinois. More advanced search revealed Ryan's shipment history over the years, the weight and description of each shipment, most of which were manual paper cutters.

The revelation was appalling but not totally surprising. Both of us were well aware of the fact it could be someone from our church since church used to be our whole social circle. I suspected Ryan a few times but told myself not to be ridiculous. Joe had collaborated with him on a few failed business endeavors during the eighteen-month unemployment period. Ryan might have justified his copycat act by convincing himself Joe should have included him in the paper cutter business and since that didn't happen, he had a right to share the success of our business. But by going to all the trouble to conceal his business and the identities of its owners for so many years, it was clear he knew he was doing something ungodly—something someone wouldn't do to his neighbors much less his brother in Christ.

After reviewing the case, Detective Johnson told us that it would be really difficult if not impossible to find out who had listed our home phone number on the porn sites. Since it looked like we would never know who did it, we just had to let it go. So we changed our phone number, made it unlisted, and moved on with our lives. I also asked the church secretary to pull our information off the printed church directory.

"It seemed to me that you should switch to a different church," Detective Johnson said to Joe half-jokingly.

"We have switched."

"I'd do the same thing."

*

Julia's battle in court was becoming too consuming and exhausting. She said to me more than once she was about to have a nervous breakdown because everyday she was worried that John would do something unthinkable to harm her or her parents. John called the police again and reported domestic violence, this time claiming Judy hit him with a tennis racket.

What made it harder was that Andy came home from school and witnessed the whole thing including the cops rebuking his mother for crying in front of her son. The next day, Andy told his mommy, "I came home happy yesterday. But everything changed after I got home." It broke Judy's heart. But the power of a mother's love for her son could never be underestimated, and it was an overwhelming source of energy and resilience for Judy. She never complained about anything or blamed anyone for the situation she was in, and she never allowed John to take away that bright smile away from her. She only blamed herself not listening to her inner voice when marrying John. Judy wasn't delusional about John either. She wasn't expecting a miracle that John one day would change and turn into a worthy husband.

After numerous court days and tens and thousands of dollars on lawyer fees, Judy won sole custody of Andy. Upon receiving half of Judy's 401K savings, John had to move out of the house. On the D-day, John asked Judy to give him a few more days because he hadn't found a place yet. Being a trusting and kind-hearted woman, Judy said OK. Then she remembered what she had been fighting for all these years. So she went back to John, "I'm afraid you'll have to move out today. You've known it for a while and so it isn't my problem that you don't have a place to stay. The deadline is 5 p.m. today. I'll have to call the police if you aren't out by then."

John did leave that day but left some of his stuff on the driveway to be picked up later. Finally, Judy could enjoy a peaceful and loving home with her son and elderly parents although at the back of her mind she still feared that John would find some way to get back at her someday.

*

Life goes on with its joy, laughter, hope, heartbreak, tears, and disappointment. Some fight for changes and others try to hold onto the past. Either way, it's a battle. For Joe and me, at times it could turn into a double battle.

We were wandering and sometimes stuck between the past and present. There were things in the past that worked well such as following the roles of the husband and wife according to the teachings of the Bible, and the reverence towards God that kept our egos in check. But Joe tossed that single handedly when he decided that the God as described in the Bible wasn't real and got me on the same page. There were things in the present that were empowering. I thought we were more open and real with each other. I no longer followed his lead because it was the Christian thing to do. When rare opportunities came up to purchase deeply discounted properties in San Diego and Joe inclined to pass, I convinced him to take the risk. We ended up buying more than one condominium; they turned out to be excellent investments. Joe no longer felt he had to do everything to make me happy because my happiness was his responsibility. He knew how much I loved going to Lifetime and how much more I'd have loved it if he went along. After working out with me for a couple of months, he started to have neck problems. I eagerly invited him to join me again after his slow recovery.

"No, you go ahead and have fun. I'm going take a longer break, OK?" He winked at me.

Instead of nagging, I continued the routine myself. Joe eventually returned a couple of times a week just to swim, but he never got up to the second floor again.

We cared for each other enough to make this new relationship work. The problem emerged when Joe and I regarded ourselves correct more often than our fair share.

"It hurts your ego when I tell you you are wrong. Admit it!" I challenged Joe when he wore that dismal look on his face.

"Am I that shallow? I could be wrong. Anybody could be wrong. I don't have a problem with that at all." He tried to force a smile.

But Joe wasn't all that deep, and I wasn't always compassionate towards him. Sometimes things got blown out of proportion when we least expected it.

We had been living in the new house for almost eight years and Joe was in charge of setting the temperature in the house. He purchased a complicated thermometer for the second floor and programmed it so that the temperature varied during the course of the day. Jane and Michelle always complained that it was too hot upstairs in the summer and often slept in the basement. The issue was their schedule was often different from how Joe programmed the thermometer. Jake frequently got sweaty in his room even when he was just listening to me reading. I had to call Joe upstairs to adjust the temperature, and he always did it willingly. One scorching summer morning as I was working from home, the cleaning lady asked me if I could lower the temperature upstairs. I got Joe on the phone, and he instructed me how to unlock the thermometer and reset the temperature. Armed with the new knowledge, I set the temperature a few degrees lower permanently. Since Joe's study and our master bedroom were on the first floor, he rarely went upstairs and therefore didn't find out until a couple of weeks later.

"Who reset the temperature upstairs? It's freezing up there. The fan has been on too. It can get burned easily." Joe's eyebrows turned into a tight knot.

"I did. I probably turned the fan on by mistake. It was just too hot."

"You know it's not trivial to set up the optimal temperature in this house? The thermometer upstairs is in the hallway. When the hallway gets above the set temperature, the air condition kicks in, and it takes a while for the whole second floor to cool down. If you set the temperature too low, the system is always on even when there is nobody upstairs. It's a waste of energy."

"All I know is when it gets too hot, you turn the air on. There is nothing complicated about that." I had no patience to listen to another lecture.

"We aren't millionaires. Lowering five degrees like you did means $200 extra a month. You can do a simple calculation to get that."

"I know we aren't millionaires. But there is nothing wrong with wanting to be comfortable at one's own home. I'd have put up with it if it were just me. But it's not OK when it gets too hot for the kids to live up there."

Before each of us realized it, we were again sucked into this dark hole that once in, not a single winner would emerge. Joe grew silent and didn't talk to me for a few days. I ignored him and pretended that nothing was wrong.

When we finally talked again, Joe said he was deeply saddened by my accusation that made him look like an evil person who purposely tried to make life miserable for his family. I couldn't understand why a simple request to turn the temperature down a notch could evolve into something like this.

"The thermometer is at least five years old. Maybe it's not working as efficiently as it's supposed to. I've ordered a new one online. A simpler one and so you can have all the control you want. So there you have it!" Joe heaved a sad sigh.

A month later, I received the water and electricity bill for a whopping $630.70. So comfort did cost money. I paid the bill quietly and turned the temperature up a couple of degrees.

I discovered a dance school next door to the martial arts studio where Jake was taking lessons. So Joe and I began taking private dance lessons, something we always wanted to do but had never found the time. Dance was fun but also caused friction between us. Joe might be smarter, wiser, and more mature, but I was definitely a better dancer. Surprisingly, Joe didn't see it that way. He would make those weird, creative, and annoying moves that threw me off. When I told him to stop and just be normal, he would command, "Just follow me. I'm supposed to lead, right? So just follow." We would exchange disapproving looks at each other when our steps were out of sync.

After a few months, our petite and elegant instructor invited us to perform rumba at the Star of the Night showcase. Joe and I worked hard practicing. Some days we looked good together, but other days I thought we were going to make fools of ourselves.

When we rehearsed on Saturday morning before the performance that night, she burst into tears and couldn't stop crying.

"That was so beautiful. You made me choke up, the way you moved so gracefully and the way you looked at smiled at each other--that's why I love my job. Sorry for being like this, but it was just so beautiful."

I gave her a big hug. "You're a great instructor. We were like idiots when we first started, do you remember?"

"Oh, no, no. You guys weren't that bad," she laughed.

One of Pastor Dale's sermons on houses built on rocks versus sand made me think. He posed the question, "What will reveal the foundation of the house?" After a deliberate pause, Dale answered his own question, "Storms of life."

*What is the foundation of our house? Can Joe and I overcome the storms of life instead of being swept away by their forces?*

So I reminded Joe of the sermon content as we headed to Banff, Canada, a little getaway over the Labor Day weekend just for the two of us.

"Are we ready for the storms of life? We used to have God, church, and a strong support system. Now it's just us. How do we know that our house is going to stand after the storm?" I wanted Joe to think about it as well.

Joe didn't have to think. He already had the answer. "The truth is no house will stand if the force is greater than what it's built to take. As for us, we can increase our resistance by communicating, understanding each other and life as general."

Our conversation didn't go very far or deep as we were going through the various check points at the airport. Little did we know that trials were awaiting us not far ahead.

Banff really lived up to its reputations. The mountains stretched hundreds of miles and embraced us from all around. The creamy green glacier lakes, creeks, and waterfalls glittered under the bright sunlight. The *National Geographic* rated the two-hundred-mile drive from Banff to Jasper the most scenic mountain roadway. It was so beautiful and tranquil, as if someone just took up the brushes and painted the perfect pictures. Joe admired the scenery with a sense of awe and was having a time of his life with his upgraded photography gear. We were half way to Jasper when Joe came back to the car making an odd comment.

"It's like the sun was so bright outside that everything appears blurry to me right now."

I didn't pay much attention to it. He kept on moving his right index finger around his eyes.

"I can't see my finger when it moves to the side. When I look ahead, the picture is distorted. It's really strange." Joe was getting frustrated and I started to understand the seriousness of the situation.

"His vision is impaired—brain tumor!" I quietly gasped to myself.

Our original plan was to take an excursion onto the surface of the Athabasca Glacier via the Massive Brewster Ice Explorer. But by the time we got there, Joe was in terrible shape. His vision hadn't restored plus now he had a splitting headache.

"I think we should just go to the hotel so that you can rest. I'll drive." I started to panic.

"No. I'll drive. I'll be OK." Joe put his head down on the steering wheel.

"No, you aren't OK. I am driving!"

"Are you sure?"

"Yes!"

We switched seats. With my heart pounding and my hands tightly gripping the wheel, I got us out of the parking lot and onto the winding and narrow mountain road. I could count with my one hand how many times I had driven on the highway in the past ten years. I wasn't a confident driver and didn't like driving. But this called for an exception.

Listening to Joe throwing up his gut into the plastic bag made the drive even harder. I told myself to focus on the road but couldn't help trying to figure out how to get us home if Joe became incapacitated.

"This must be altitude illness. My vision is getting better," Joe informed me between his forceful vomits.

I took a deep breath of relief. *Thank goodness it's not a brain tumor—and thank goodness for GPS!* An hour and a half later we arrived at our hotel at Jasper. The young lady behind the reception desk told me our room wouldn't be available until 4 p.m., which meant we had to wait another hour and a half.

I demanded a room, "My husband is sick, and he needs to lie down right now."

"Okay, in that case I'll switch you to a different room."

I checked us in. Joe went straight to bed.

When I put the steamy Ramen cup in his hand, he looked at me lovingly. "Did you know that you saved my life today? I would have had died if you weren't there."

"No, you would have had made it."

"I don't know. The headache almost killed me."

"I thought it was a brain tumor when you were experiencing vision problems, but I didn't tell you."

"What if it were brain tumor?"

"Hopefully, you wouldn't die today. I'll have to try to get us home."

Joe smiled again. "You acted pretty calm through the whole thing."

"But I panicked inside."

In about an hour, Joe announced that he was well enough to explore Jasper. The brief storm of life passed. Both of us were still standing, but not for too long.

Jasper was as breathtaking as Banff. Joe bounced back to his old energetic and enthusiastic self as if nothing had happened. At Maligne Lake, while moving his tripod around on the deck to capture the picture-perfect scene, Joe stepped into a narrow rotten wood plank and got his foot stuck between the adjacent planks. He couldn't move. Luckily an Indian couple was also on the deck taking pictures. The guy lent a foot and after some maneuvering set Joe free. Joe's foot was bruised, swollen, and he had to walk with a limp for the rest of the evening. He needed ice but we didn't know where to get it. Being a resourceful guy, Joe dipped his foot in the ice-cold glacier lake. The next day the limp went away, and he was as good as new.

On the way to Jasper downtown after the foot incident, the GPS issued a low-battery warning. Joe realized the rental car charger had stopped working. Instead of having a good meal in a cozy restaurant, we spent the evening limping around searching for a mini cable so that the GPS could be charged in the hotel room.

The pharmacy didn't have it, and neither did the video store or the cell phone store. Finally we found it at a camera store. When we returned to the hotel that night I was glad the day was over.

It took us more than ten hours to drive back to Banff from Jasper. Joe's altitude illness didn't come back. We made so many stops to see the things we missed on the way to Jasper. The glacier excursion was awesome. We were standing on ice that was three hundred meters deep. I was just happy that nobody was sick, injured, and we weren't caught off-guard by something unexpected. The gorgeous warmer weather and the stunning views made the ride even more pleasing. I wished every day could be as enjoyable and worry-free as this one.

The next day after a delicious dim sum brunch in Chinatown, we headed to the airport. I was expecting a trouble-free flight back home. Joe presented our passports to the officer in the booth. He asked us a couple of questions and then handed the passports back to us. We were still by the booth putting things away when a young blond woman officer in a ponytail approached us.

"Follow me. This way, please." She gestured us to turn right.

Joe and I walked behind her, making faces at each other.

"What do you have in that gray hard case?" she asked with a flat tone of voice.

"Oh, it's my photography equipment."

We were led to a small and enclosed area with a long table in the middle. The officer motioned for us to place everything on the table.

"Do you have any food with you?"

"Oh, yes, yes. I've got some fruit with me that I'm going to eat on the airplane." Joe stuttered.

My heard dropped. I had suggested to him to throw the rest of the fresh longan away. But Joe sounded one hundred percent positive when he replied, "This is still Canada. They don't care if you take food with you. As long as I don't have it when we land in the U.S., it's not going to be a problem."

I remembered we were asked to eat the bananas or throw them away when we were departing the airport in Hawaii. So I brought it up again. Joe offered the same answer.

The customs officer disagreed with Joe. "Do you know you're going to screw up our agriculture by doing this?"

"I was going to eat it on the airplane. I didn't know we were going through customs on the Canadian side. This is Canada, right?" Joe chortled.

The blond officer wasn't amused. She pointed at the customs form Joe had filled out. "You checked the 'no' box to the food category. You should have checked 'yes' and been honest."

Now that she had proved our guilt, she went through everything in our luggage and bombarded us with interrogational questions.

"How much money do you have with you?"

"A couple hundred dollars." I answered.

"I—I am not sure." Joe reached for his pocket.

"Just give me an estimate. I don't need you to count it." She gave Joe a stern look.

"Maybe five hundred?"

Seeing a white gift box with the red word "Canada" on it, she opened it. Inside there were a hand-painted pendant and a pair of matching earrings made of aluminum I bought in downtown Banff.

"How many gifts did you buy?"

I didn't know how much Joe put down for gifts, and being fully aware that the blond was ready to pounce on us any minute, my survival instinct kicked in. I decided to go low.

"Fifty dollars."

In the end, she didn't find anything else on us.

"Wait here and I'll be back. And you can pack up your suitcases now." She left with our passports.

Ten minutes later, the officer reappeared with our documents.

"Truly sorry about that. I really didn't mean to take the food to Chicago. I apologize. Please don't put us on the black list." Joe made a last ditch effort to salvage a bad situation.

The blonde didn't buy into any of it. "We're here to do a job. I can't tell you what I have or haven't put into your record."

"I'm really sorry. Please understand." Joe wasn't going to give up.

"Let's just go!" I started walking with one of the suitcases.

We were stopped again when our carry-ons were going through the conveyor belt. The x-ray revealed something suspicious inside Joe's backpack. I was confident we were clean since the officer had already looked through all our stuff. But surprise, surprise, they found a nifty sharp knife we bought in Calgary that I used to peel apples for Joe.

"You should have known not to put the knife in the carry-on bag," I groaned under my breath. I handed him the knife the night before when we were packing.

"I thought I had put it in the checked bag. I'm almost sure I did," Joe mumbled.

"But it's not there. It's here." I no longer tried to hide my disappointment.

"We can UPS it to you if you want. All you have to do is fill out the form over there." The security lady was much more friendly and understanding.

The knife cost $12. "Just toss it." Joe waved his hand and smiled at the kind lady.

We got to the gate without any more problems. I sat down, silent and stone-faced.

"So you are mad." Joe glanced at me.

"I told you to throw the fruit away. What if she did make a note in the system? Now they'll go through our bags every time we come back from China. What a pain! And why did you put the knife in the backpack?" I complained.

"So it's all my fault?"

I thought about it for a minute. "Come to think of it, yeah, it's your fault." I said calmly.

"Okay. It's my fault, I screwed up. If you like that knife so much, I'll buy you another one. I'll buy ten of them."

"I don't want that knife." I stared into his eyes and then looked away.

Neither of us spoke another word for the rest of the trip.

"So we failed the test," Joe broke the silence after we got home and settled in bed after midnight.

"I guess so."

"I felt wronged by that customs officer. I needed comfort and understanding at the time. But you blamed me, too. It made me feel even worse. When I hurt my foot, you didn't even care to take a look at it. I don't know, I feel lonely and cold."

I had the tendency to withdraw when things got too stressful. Joe interpreted that as uncaring. But I was in no mood to explain or carry on a lengthy conversation because I checked my email after we got home and found out that I had to go to the office in the morning instead of working from home, which meant I had to get up in less than five hours. However, a profound shift took place that moment: Joe was actually sharing with me his deep, internal feelings. "I feel lonely and cold," didn't sound like anything from Joe's mouth. I was used to him saying things like "I'm OK" and "Everything is fine," even when they weren't. My heart instantly softened and a shot of warmth went up and down my spine. *But it's too late and we'll have to hash this out tomorrow*, I told myself.

We made up the sweet Joe-and-Linda style the next day, and I woke up with a song in my heart. Joe started sending me text messages quoting Chinese idioms and poems proclaiming his love for me and subtly expressing a desire for a more intimate and harmonious relationship. I texted him back, "U r so full of it but I love all the same."

I was even more shocked when Joe told me that he had spent the last few days searching for an experienced and credible counselor to help us improve our communication skills. I suggested seeking counseling before when we were contemplating divorce, but Joe took it as an insult.

"I'm fifty years old. Why do I need counseling? What can they tell me that I don't already know?" he grunted indignantly.

But now Joe himself had placed phone calls to Northwestern University and inquired about their counseling services and rates. At the end Joe being the "quality, comfort, and affordability guy," figured that traveling an hour and a half to Northwestern one way and paying an hourly rate of at least $180 wasn't worth it, so he ordered more than a dozen of books on the subject.

"Let's see what the bright minds have to say," Joe chuckled. "Baby, I really want us to communicate better. I want us to stand together to face the storms of life. Will you be on this journey with me?"

My heart rejoiced. "Of course, I'll be on this journey with you!"

"So how about I read these three books and you read those, and we'll discuss and learn and get better at this, right?"

Dr. Phil wrote the books he handed me. I loved the titles *Family First* and *Relationship Rescue*.

"Right! I'll read them all. And of course we'll discuss and learn and improve."

No, we didn't pass the test with flying colors. And no, my dear Joe wasn't as perfect as I thought he was, and my flaws were even more obvious. But if awareness was the first step to awakening and willingness to learn and change the catalyst for life-changing transformation, we were moving in the right direction and readying ourselves for whatever was awaiting us in the near or far future.

\*

Looking down at the lingering, yet majestic, thick clouds, and the buildings, roads, cars, and trees turning into little dots underneath, I was reminded once again how insignificant each of us really was in the big realm of things.

I was on my way to Shanghai to attend my cousin Catherine's wedding, the first family wedding in the past twenty-some years. My mother was turning eighty this month. Over the years, the relationship between mother and me had changed from hostile to a polite and yet distant one. I asked Yiwen to ask her how she wanted to celebrate her big birthday. I suggested we do it the Chinese way by inviting family and friends to have a feast in a nice restaurant. Yiwen came back and delivered the message: mother wished to take a cruise vacation with some of her friends and wanted to know if I would pay for it. And I did. The ship took mother to Japan and Korea, but she and her friends spent more time standing in lines than having fun, and so she didn't think it was worth the money.

Catherine is the only daughter of my oldest uncle, the one who was dressed like a girl by Grandma. Big uncle hadn't made an effort to stay close to his side of the family, and he and his wife left the rest of my family in the guessing by not officially inviting them to the big event until three weeks before the ceremony. My two cousins who lived in Australia and Singapore weren't informed at all. Catherine asked me to purchase a diamond ring for her in the U.S., and therefore Joe and I had the honor of receiving the formal invitation six months ahead.

Catherine attended a technical school after high school and, to my knowledge, had never worked a single day in her life. Her new husband's family resided in Mexico and sold small merchandise made in China. As far as I knew he didn't have a real job either. The wedding banquet was hosted at a European style clubhouse in Shanghai Xijiao with about one hundred guests.

Shortly after we arrived at big uncle's home after an hour ride in the taxi, his wife directed the guests waiting there to get on a hired tour bus that would take us to the clubhouse. Another hour later, we reached the destination.

We were led to the top floor of the four-story clubhouse. Pinkish fresh flower arrangements were placed along the hallway leading to the banquet hall. Inside the hall, there were stained glass windows on both sides and European style paintings on the domed ceiling. A couple of chandeliers dazzled magnificently, adding a glow to everything beneath: the silver chopsticks and spoons, the chopstick holders, the round golden candy boxes, the flower vases on each table, the golden bows wrapped around the back of the chairs with the white cover. The scene from the balcony was lovely further complimented by the unusually mild October weather in Shanghai.

I saw the bride standing outside the banquet hall when I came down the stairs from the balcony. She looked absolutely stunning in a white embroidered wedding gown with a delicate flower-edged, floor-length veil. Her big diamond ring sparkled brightly, and she had a wide cuff gold bracelet on each wrist. I hugged Catherine, and she thanked me for coming all the way from America to attend her wedding.

The whole ceremony was a not-so-natural mixture of Eastern and Western traditions. I wasn't sure if the handsome emcee was a family friend or a professional. When he had to look at a small piece of paper to pronounce the groom's name, I realized he must be hired. The lights were dimmed when the bride walked in with her father in the dancing spotlights. There were vow exchanges, speeches from the father of the bride, the bride, and the groom, as well as games and prize drawing. It was surprising that the parents of the groom couldn't make it to the ceremony. Only two representatives from his side of the family were present. The bride and groom weren't in the banquet hall most of the evening. They disappeared after the symbolic kiss and reappeared briefly after half of the dozen main dishes had been served. This time the bride changed into a red ballroom gown. They cut the cake and thanked their parents for raising and supporting them. Catherine burst into tears as she and her mother hugged each other.

The games played in the absence of the bride and groom had nothing to do with new couple. It was just for fun, like guessing the name of the song or dancing spontaneously to the music. I didn't find out how Catherine met and fell in love with her husband or hear any stories told by their friends. No slide show was presented, and to my great disappointment there was no wedding dance. The food kept on coming and was good by my standard, but everyone else thought it wasn't very fresh. The whole banquet lasted about three hours. The emcee was also a singer who performed for the guests.

The new couple came back again towards the end to go around each table and show gratitude to every guest. This time Catherine wore a yellow nightgown. This was typically the time when the bride and groom were challenged to drink and *ganbei* (bottom up).

Uncle DD revealed his other side after having a few more drinks than he should have and was going around the tables making bold comments. "*Ganbei, ganbei!*" He lifted his glass. "What? This table is running out of wine? That's a disgrace. It's my brother's fault. He's the big lawyer. He makes a ton of money out of the plaintiffs and then turns around to make more from the defendants. He can afford more alcohol for his daughter's wedding. Ha-ha-ha!"

Uncle DD approached the honorary table seated by the bride's parents and close family members. "There is something I don't understand. Where are the groom's parents? My niece came all the way back from America to attend this wedding. Which country are they in that they can't be here today?"

Big uncle's wife was getting uncomfortable. She whispered to Uncle DD's wife to get her husband under control who in turn pulled my uncle away and brought him back to his own table.

The wedding appeared well rehearsed and controlled but somehow lacked the elements of fun and the free spirit of celebration and joy of two lives merging together. The groom looked handsome and happy, but in his speeches, he was almost apologetic for not being as successful as he was expected to be and promised that he would try harder to offer a happy and prosperous life for Catherine.

I was glad I made the trip back for Catherine's big day. I had the opportunity to reconnect with many relatives I hadn't seen for a very long time. Some still remembered me as a baby or toddler. Most importantly I connected with my mother the way I had never been able to before.

Mother and I sat at the same table at the wedding. She still had a full head of grayish hair at the age of eighty. Her fresh perm made her look younger and energetic. She wore a black cardigan outside a green and brown half turtleneck top, quite stylish compared to the way she used to look.

"I used to always save my nice clothes for later. But I'm eighty years old. There is not too much later left," Mother declared happily to anyone who commented on her nice and modern look. What struck me most was the warmth that characterized her demeanor instead of bitterness and anger. Mother glanced at me from time to time with a loving smile and I smiled back.

"Hey, Lao Ma, (mom in Shanghainese), it's your birthday. Can I take you out for lunch or dinner?" I went over to her and asked.

Mom didn't expect that, but she was visibly thrilled.

"Don't waste your money like that. But OK, yes. OK, yes."

"Where do you want to go?"

"I'll go wherever you choose!"

On a warm, breezy, and sunny day when the sky behind the clouds was almost blue, Mother and I got into a hot pot restaurant in Pudong for lunch. The place wasn't crowded, and we were seated in a booth at the back. There was a period of silence as we hid behind the screen created by the steam coming from the hot pots. Then mother spoke. "You know, Hongwei, I've made lots of mistakes in my life, but the one I regretted most was how I mistreated you," her voice cracked. "I wanted you to accept me so badly that I ..."

"Mom, I no longer hate you for that. I was stubborn and hostile towards you, which didn't make things easy." I saw tears welled up in mother's eyes behind the smoke screen.

"The years we stayed in Yun Nan were damn hard. I was tormented that I couldn't be with my children, but your father needed me. I thought I'd gave you a better chance with life by sending you to Shanghai." Mother's lips quivered as she spoke between sobs.

I reached out and put my hand on hers. "That turned out to be the right decision, and I'm grateful for your sacrifice."

Mother smiled with tears flooding down her cheeks. I looked at her with moist eyes and smiled too.

*

"Mommy, Daddy, do you know that Jesus is up in the sky behind the clouds?" Jake announced from the backseat as we were on our way home.

I looked up. Vibrant and rosy colors filled the autumn sky, and the sun was about to drop down out of the clouds.

"Jakey, how do you know Jesus is up there?" Joe sat up and looked at Jake's reflection from the front mirror.

"I learned from Sunday school at Compass. I'm serious. It's real, Dad!"

"But Jake, have you thought about—"

I looked at Joe and put my right index finger on my lips. "Let the boy figure it out himself," I whispered.

"Okay, Jakey. That's good to know." Joe looked in the mirror again and grinned.

I no longer know for sure whether the God I once believed in is as true as it's described in the Bible. I have my doubts. But I am living, every minute of it, with the man I love and the three children I adore.

*This picture was taken in Shanghai for our 10$^{th}$ anniversary*

*Celebrating 10$^{th}$ anniversary on a cruise ship*

*Renewing vows in 2001*

*Vow Renewal ceremony*

## 212  Let Go

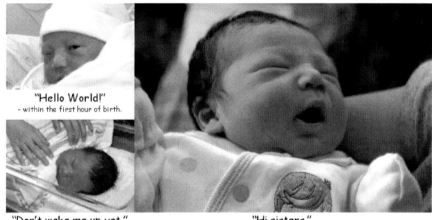

*Jake was born*

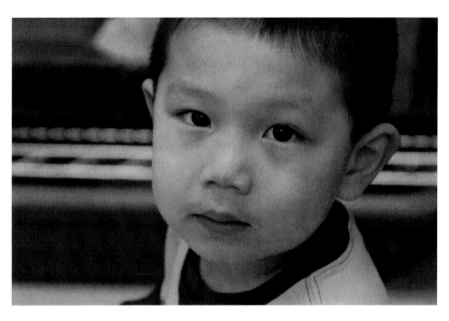

*Jake at the age of four*

*2011 family Christmas photo*

*Girls posing for the camera*

*With my children on my birthday 2012*

*Visiting Gjyn, Mitch and Esther in New Castle, Australia, 2012*

*Joe and I in Banff, Canada*

*With my mother and Uncle Mao Mao at my cousin Catherine's wedding*